Ex

It was *ex machina* ('by crane') that
the gods arrived in Greek Theatre to untangle
a hopelessly overcomplicated plot.

David J. Lee

Marshall Pickering

Acknowledgments

Thanks are due to all those who, knowingly or unknowingly, have acted as guinea pigs for the scripts collected in this book. Their sufferings are beyond measure. More particularly I am indebted to George (bless his little green face), to the members of *Ministry of Offense*, and to one trusted critic who has never been afraid to tell me I'm wrong. I frequently am.

Marshall Morgan and Scott
Marshall Pickering
34–42 Cleveland Street, London, W1P 5FB. U.K.

First published in 1989 by Marshall Morgan and Scott Publications Ltd
Part of the Marshall Pickering Holdings Group

British Library CIP Data

Lee, David
Ex machina
I. Title
822'.914

ISBN. 0 551 01834 8

Text Set in Baskerville by Avocet Robinson, Buckingham
Printed in Great Britain by Cox & Wyman Ltd. Reading

Contents

deus ex machina?

Join one of Britain's more progressive congregations on a Sunday morning and you are likely to find the ministry of the Word backed up by the ministry of the Act; in other words, a sketch.

The skills necessary to execute this hybrid form of drama, which generally owes more to the revue tradition than to Shakespeare or Noël Coward, are passed down by means of another now time-honoured institution: the workshop. What results is travesty or light relief, according to your point of view. But only rarely does it qualify as art in the accepted and slightly snobby sense of the term. Most of the performers would not think of themselves as actors, nor would many regard the successful performance of the sketch as an end in itself. Drama, in church-speak, now denotes the use of certain theatrical forms to communicate the Christian faith. It is ideologically motivated.

For the scriptwriter, accommodating ideology can result in a kind of tightrope act. In most cases you don't want to be too explicit or preachy; but then again the occasions on which drama is required nearly always call upon it to make a statement, or at least ask a question. Just to be funny, or just to be provocative, isn't enough; something has to be said. Add to that the need to assume a minimum of acting ability in the players, not to mention an acute shortage of rehearsal time, and the scriptwriter realizes he has set himself a task much like scaling the north face of the Eiger.

But so much for the excuses. This particular collection

of scripts has been written with two aims in mind. First, and contrary to the advice of Abraham Lincoln, I have made a strenuous attempt to please everyone. The pieces are not uniformly demanding; some are very easy, others quite difficult; some can read, others need to be learned. They cover a range of themes, for the most part explained in the introductions, and employ a variety of dramatic forms ranging from simple oratory to dance. What they have in common – at least what I hope they have in common – is a style and humour in keeping with the times; which accounts for the high profile of satire as a comic technique and the presence of experimental pieces like BOATING FOR GOPHERS, a four-part rap.

Second, thought has been given to the venues in which drama of this kind is performed. The church is only one of many; others include the school, the university, and the shopping mall. It may be that a sketch is not performed at all, but only used as a break from the usual routine for Sunday school, or as a starter for discussion in a youth group. Each situation has its own dramatic limitations and potentials, and each favours a certain kind of script. Sketches that assume a sedentary audience, for example, do not lend themselves to use as street theatre, nor can the rabble-rousing methods of the open-air actor be tolerated easily within the confines of Evensong. Far be it from me, of course, to cramp your style; but if you do want to match your venue to one of *ex machina*'s twenty-five scripts you can save yourself a tedious search by consulting the table at the back of the book.

And now, some good news for the criminals. You may have noticed in works similar to this one a plea from the author that you pay him a licence fee before you put the sketches on stage. Such conditions are apt to go the way of international arms treaties, and for the same reason; lack of verification. So let's be frank with one another. High though my regard is for your Christian character, I am not fool enough to believe that you will pay me £20 for the privilege of performing what you can – safely if illegally – perform completely free of charge. I'm not even going to make you feel guilty about it. All I ask is that instead of feeding this book into the nearest photocopier you go back to the shop and buy another one. If you do, you'll strike a blow for justice and make a poor writer extremely happy; if not – then a plague on you, and may your 10p jam in the machine.

Finally, a few comments about the scripts themselves. I have to make the customary apology to women readers (and I make it sincerely) for using the masculine pronoun where a character's sex is indeterminate. Though I toyed with substituting 'he/she' and 'his/hers', I rejected the idea as too clumsy, and went to 'he' and 'his' not through sexism but because – the English language being as it is – 'he' and 'his' are the more general terms.

For the purposes of directing the sketches I am assuming you have access to no more specialized equipment than a piece of empty floor. Locational direction is therefore minimal and basic; you are off stage, centre stage, stage left or stage right, towards the front or towards the back. In the cases where instructions about position and gesture are highly specific, this is either because it is important for the sense of the script or because it makes the script easier to interpret. But this should not be seen as sacrosanct. If the given directions don't work for you, ignore them and think of something else. It is, after all, my most enduring conviction about Christian theatre that it should be fun, and that your enjoyment – free from any niggling objections from the writer – should communicate to the audience.

In the end it may be your enjoyment, as much as the 'message', that strikes home.

Presidents Elect

Characters: 4
Performance time: 4 minutes

No higher science has been developed by mankind than that of the advertizing campaign. The domain of the brothers Saatchi now extends to political parties. But for the ordinary punter like you and me, having to choose between glossy, off-the-shelf policy packages raises a problem. For whom, or for what, are we really voting?

(Enter PR MAN and PRESIDENT. The PRESIDENT is holding a box with POWER *written on it, and wearing a Presidential hat)*

PR MAN: Ladies and gentlemen! Roll on up and gather round! You don't know how lucky you are to be here today! Because, ladies and gentlemen, it is my inestimable, incontrovertible, ineluctable –

PRESIDENT: Get on with it!

PR MAN: *pleasure* to introduce to you his Excellency, *ancienne noblesse* of the *hoi poloi*, king of the *mobile vulgus*, the Worshipful, Honourable, DSO and bar –

PRESIDENT: All right, all right!

PR MAN: Ladies and gentlemen, the President of the World!

(He leads applause, which the PRESIDENT greedily acknowledges)

PRESIDENT: Thank you, thank you! *(To a member of the audience)*: Yes, sir, you may get down on your knees if you wish. That's what freedom is for!

PR MAN: Ladies and gentlemen, this is a sad day in the life of the President.

PRESIDENT: *(Turning)*: It *is*?

PR MAN: It is the day on which he is required to yield up the sceptre of his power, and submit to the ballot box!

PRESIDENT: *(Horrified)*: Give away my power?

PR MAN: Of course, That's democracy. Remember?

PRESIDENT: *(Clutching the box protectively)*: Never!

PR MAN: *(Patiently)*: Come along.

PRESIDENT: Shan't!

PR MAN: *(Suddenly pointing):* Wow! Look! A missile!

PRESIDENT: Where?

(The PR MAN grabs the box, which the PRESIDENT then tries to snatch back)

PR MAN: No you don't!

PRESIDENT: Oh! Now what am I going to do?

PR MAN: You'll have to win it back.

PRESIDENT: Win it back? How can I win it back?

PR MAN: Use your loaf, Mr President.

PRESIDENT: Loaf? Loaf? You're talking to me about *loaf*? I don't even have any dough!

PR MAN: Then you'll need . . .

PRESIDENT: Yes, of course!

PR MAN: Ladies and gentlemen, a very big hand for the Presidential aides!

(Enter, to applause, LIES and HONESTY, duly labelled. They stand one on each side of the PRESIDENT)

PR MAN: Look a tricky pair to me!

LIES: *(Shaking hands intensely with the PRESIDENT)*: Hello, Mr President. And may I say what a deep, deep, deep, deep honour it is to work with you. I mean that with all my heart.

PRESIDENT: Spoken like a true friend. *(He makes to greet HONESTY, but LIES still has hold of his hand, and pulls him back)*

LIES: Never mind about him. What's the problem?

PRESIDENT: It's . . . well, it's . . . *(He points at the box, and suddenly breaks down)*: It's too painful to talk about.

PR MAN: He's got to win back his power.

LIES: You mean he wants these people to vote for him?

PRESIDENT: Yes . . . please!

LIES: Elections are my speciality. First lesson: Public Image. Strike a pose, Mr President!

(The PRESIDENT strikes a sagging pose)

No, no, no! You've got to look smart. *(He proceeds to give instructions, which the PRESIDENT follows with clumsy enthusiasm)*: Stand up straight! Throw back your shoulders! And bare those teeth in a smile! *(To the PRESIDENT, without giving the audience time to reply)*: See? They love it. Suckers!

PRESIDENT: But what do I say?

LIES: Say! You're going to try *saying* something?

PR MAN: He needs ideas.

LIES: Ideas, okay. Let's have a look. *(He pulls some cards from his pocket)*: See what they make of this one. *(Slowly)*: I'll cut taxes by fifty percent.

PRESIDENT: *(Mimicking with gusto)*: I'll cut taxes by fifty percent!

(The PR MAN leads a cheer)

LIES: I'll feed the world's poor.

PRESIDENT: I'll feed the world's poor!

(The PR MAN leads a cheer)

LIES: I'll get rid of the Bomb.

PRESIDENT: I'll get rid of the Bomb!

(The PR MAN leads a cheer)

HONESTY: *(Who until now has been watching anxiously)*: Wait! Do you mean that?

PRESIDENT: Mean what?

HONESTY: That you'll cut taxes, feed the poor, get rid of the Bomb?

PRESIDENT; Er – no, I don't.

LIES: That's my boy!

HONESTY: So what *are* you going to do if they vote for you?

PRESIDENT: Well, I think I'll –

LIES: *(Clapping a hand over the PRESIDENT's mouth)*: Careful! Second lesson: Don't boob it up in front of the media!

HONESTY: *(To the audience)*: Did you see that? He's lying! The man is lying through his teeth!

LIES: Shut up, you fool!

HONESTY: Why should I?

LIES: Do you want to lose us our jobs?

HONESTY: These people have a right to know.

LIES: *(Pullling a gun)*: And I have a right not to tell them!

(He shoots HONESTY, who falls dead. The PRESIDENT removes his hat in respect. During the PR MAN's speech LIES

replaces the gun, walks round behind the PRESIDENT, and placing his hands on his shoulders, slowly and firmly pushes him down to his knees. LIES then takes and dons the Presidential hat)

PR MAN: And now for a free democratic election! The candidates are – in the red corner: truth, love, freedom and all the values you thought would make the world a better place; then in the blue corner: His Excellency, *ancienne noblesse* of the *hoi poloi*, king of the *mobile vulgus*, the Worshipful, Honourable DSO and bar –

LIES: Get on with it!

PR MAN: The President of the World! Vote for him and he's yours. Get ready, ladies and gentlemen. All those wishing to return the President to office prepare to raise your right hands and shout 'Aye'! One, two . . . *(But he breaks off just as LIES is about to shout)*: On second thoughts, ladies and gentlemen, this is not a time for hasty decisions. Please collect your ballot papers and return them here next year. And remember – *(Holding up the box)*: in the meantime, *this* is *yours*! (*He throws the box into the audience*)

The Babblers Build a Tower

Characters: 4 principals, 3 to 15 others
Performance time: 4 minutes

It was once said of the Kingdom of God that ' . . . the violent take it by force' (Matthew 11:12). The principle is aptly illustrated in the Babel story, and echoed in the third temptation of Christ. But of course the heavenly Kingdom cannot be inherited by flesh and blood; only bestowed as a divine gift. God's grace is not Babel, but Pentecost.

That distinction is the subject of THE BABBLERS BUILD A TOWER. Although the sketch was written for children, it actually works just as well with adults. Perhaps that says more about the adults than they'd care to admit? Either way the words aren't exactly hard to remember . . .

(The BABBLERS are lying around, snoring, among a dozen or so cardboard boxes. On a step ladder towards the back of the stage sits GOD. THUMBSCROO, who is carrying a large book, takes up his position to stage left, and is preparing to speak when SNOTT hurries on. SNOTT is what the Americans call 'gung-ho')

SNOTT: *(Oozing naive enthusiasm)*: Hi! What's going on?

THUMBSCROO: I'm telling a story.

SNOTT: *(Surveying the BABBLERS)*: It can't be very exciting – they're all asleep;

THUMBSCROO: I haven't started yet.

SNOTT: It's not the one about Superman meets Thomas the Tank Engine is it? I've heard that before.

THUMBSCROO: No. It's about the Babblers.

SNOTT: Babblers!

THUMBSCROO: They were called Babblers because they couldn't stop talking.

SNOTT: Wow! My sort of people!

THUMBSCROO: A bit worse than you. Because in those days there was only one word to say.

(The BIG BABBLER suddenly jumps up)

BIG BABBLER: *(Loudly)* Blah!

(Suddenly woken, the BABBLERS assemble in a line towards the front of the stage, standing to attention. The BIG BABBLER gets up on a box, stage right, and inspects them)

SNOTT: Who's that?

THUMBSCROO: He's called the Big Babbler – he talks more than anyone else.

BIG BABBLER: Blah, bla-a-ah *blah!*

(Immediately after the final 'blah' the BABBLERS

stamp their right feet and salute briefly, in unison)

SNOTT: What's he doing?

THUMBSCROO: He's taking a roll call.

(The BIG BABBLER gives a sharp double handclap, after which each BABBLER, starting with the one closest to the BIG BABBLER, responds with a 'blah')

BABBLERS: *(In order, and in varying pitches)*: Blah!

SNOTT: That's impressive!

THUMBSCROO: Now comes the speech.

BIG BABBLER: Blah, blah, blah . . .

THUMBSCROO: 'Friends, Babblers, countrymen . . . '

BIG BABBLER: blah, blah, blah, blah, blah . . .

THUMBSCROO: 'today we will build a tower so high . . . '

BIG BABBLER: blah, blah, blah, *blah!*

THUMBSCROO: ' . . . that it will take us to heaven!'

(A round of applause from the BABBLERS)

SNOTT: Wow! That's going to be some tower!

(The BIG BABBLER promptly sets up a chant)

BIG BABBLER: Blah, blah, *blah!* Blah, blah, *blah!*

(The BABBLERS take it up)

BABBLERS: Blah, blah, *blah!* Blah, blah, *blah!*

(Still chanting, the BABBLERS scatter to collect the boxes. When they return to the line they pass the boxes one to another in the direction of the BIG BABBLER, who piles them up in a heap. Every BABBLER who has ceased to pass boxes immediately stands to attention, but carries on with the chant until the heap is completed and the BIG BABBLER, himself now standing to attention, motions that it should be cut)

SNOTT: Have they got to heaven yet?

THUMBSCROO: Almost. They're going to finish it tomorrow.

BIG BABBLER: Blah!

(The BABBLERS and the BIG BABBLER immediately lie down and begin to snore)

THUMBSCROO: But who do you think showed up in the middle of the night?

SNOTT: The tooth fairy?

THUMBSCROO: No.

SNOTT: Dracula?

THUMBSCROO: I'll give you a clue – he lives in heaven.

SNOTT: My Uncle Bill.

THUMBSCROO: No, not your Uncle Bill – God!

(GOD comes down from the step ladder and picks his way over the sleeping BABBLERS to inspect the tower)

See – there he is. And God checked out the tower and said:

GOD: *(To the audience):* They're coming to see me on *that*?

SNOTT: Tomorrow morning, God. They've almost finished it.

GOD: Hm. I think they could use some help here.

SNOTT: How are you going to help them?

GOD: Just wait and see!

(GOD promptly re-ascends the step ladder and sits again)

SNOTT: What happened next?

THUMBSCROO: The sun rose, and morning came.

(The BIG BABBLER suddenly stands)

BIG BABBLER: *(Loudly)*: Blah!

(Once again the BABBLERS get up and stand to attention. The BIG BABBLER gets up on his box to inspect the line)

SNOTT: It must be roll call time again.

BIG BABBLER: Blah bla-a-ah *blah!*

(As before, immediately after the final 'blah' the BABBLERS stamp their right feet and salute in unison. The BIG BABBLER gives the double handclap to call the roll, and the BABBLERS respond in order as they did before. But this time they all say different words)

BABBLERS: *(Variously)*: Boom! Bick! Bog! Bunk! Blip! Bap! Biff! Boop! Bolley! Bat! Bonk!

(As each BABBLER hears himself say the wrong word he brings his hand down from the salute and claps it over his mouth. Finally, with the whole line standing hand over mouth, the BIG BABBLER covers his ears and grimaces. They all freeze)

SNOTT: They're speaking different languages!

THUMBSCROO: They couldn't understand each other.

SNOTT: What did they do?

THUMBSCROO: What would *you* do if nobody understood you?

SNOTT: I don't know, I think I'd–panic!

(On the word 'panic' the BABBLERS run to the

tower. Shouting his own word each grabs a box, puts it down on the floor and sits on it with his arms over his head. God stretches, climbs down from his ladder, and comes to the front of the stage, dusting his palms in satisfaction)

SNOTT: So they never got to heaven?

THUMBSCROO: Not with the tower.

SNOTT: But God – I thought you were going to help them!

GOD: I did help them. Now what was that word?

SNOTT: Blah.

(The BABBLERS, including the BIG BABBLER, immediately get up and form a line)

GOD: No one ever got to heaven by building towers. If you want to get to heaven, you'll have to follow me. I think that makes a good moral for the story, don't you?

SNOTT: Beats the one in Superman meets Thomas the Tank Engine. That's for sure.

THUMBSCROO: Which leaves only one more thing to say . . .

EVERYONE: Blah, blah!

GOD: The end.

Santa Who?

Characters: 4
Performance time: 3 minutes

To the popular imagination God and Santa Claus have a lot in common. Both belong to the world of the supernatural; both live in remote, fantastic places; and to judge by their beards, both are past retirement. Neither has much contribution to make to everyday life, with the result that for 360 days of the year they are studiously ignored by everyone except (on the one hand) the Christian church and (on the other) frenetic salesmen devising next season's yuletide gimmick. We no longer expect either God or Santa Claus to put in a personal appearance at Christmas. If they did we probably wouldn't recognize them anyway . . .

(Enter MAGICIAN, SIDEKICKS standing to his left. He addresses the children)

MAGICIAN: Magic trick time! Who'd like a great magician to do a magic trick? *(If no one responds)*: Okay, let's put it another way. Who'd like a free Christmas present? Good. That's more like it. Now first of all I need to know something. Who is the funny man with the white beard who comes down your chimney on Christmas Eve?

(If you haven't accidentally started the sketch in front of a bunch of Japanese

tourists, one child will probably oblige with the answer)

Correct! *(Aside, to the audience in general)*: I tell you, this kid's going to go far. *(To the child)*:What would you say if I told you I could bring Santa here, right now? I don't mean any of those second-rate Santas upstairs in Selfridges, with the Wellington boots on. The real Santa. Would you like that? *(If the child doesn't cooperate)*: He might just give you a present . . . Yes, I thought that'd get to you. Okay. For this we need a magic wand . . .

(SECOND SIDEKICK hands him a wooden spoon)

. . . thank you. *(To the child)*: If you'd just like to hold on to this. And . . . an ordinary pocket handkerchief. Hold it up, please.

(FIRST SIDEKICK produces a sheet. The SIDEKICKS hold the sheet up as a screen, behind which SANTA dons a red bobble cap, beard, dark glasses and cigar)

That's lovely. Take it from me, you wouldn't want to meet the bloke who blows his nose on *that*. Finally, some magic words. *(To the child)*: Can you think of any magic words? What does

Santa say when he's happy? *Ho, ho, ho!* That's right. Think we can all say that? Let's practice. One, two, three four –

ALL BUT SANTA: *Ho, ho, ho!*

FIRST SIDEKICK: . . . and a bottle of rum. Sixteen men on a dead man's chest, ho, ho, ho . . .

(The singing peters out under the MAGICIAN's glare)

MAGICIAN: Santa Claus, not Long John Silver. We'll do it again. And after we've said it, you wave the wand. One, two, three, four –

ALL BUT SANTA: *Ho, ho, ho!*

(When the child waves the wand the sheet is removed, revealing SANTA)

SANTA: *(Doing an inept cabaret performance):*

Oh, you'd better watch out,
You'd better not cry,
You'd better not pout –
I'm telling you why . . .
Santa Claus is coming to town,
(Ba-jeeba-dooba, ba-jeeba-doo-da!)

(He finishes frozen in an Astaire pose, and the MAGICIAN leads applause. SANTA then claps and rubs his hands)

Ha, ha! So where's the kid with the wand? You did a grand job. 'Cept would you mind holding it round the other way next time 'cause I don't usually smoke cigars, know what I mean? Now who wants a present? C'mon, hands up. Who wants a present? Aha – just as I thought! *(Reaching for his bag)*: It just so happens I have with me a whole bag full of live jellyfish. Purple and slimy with one heck of a big sting. Who wants to be first to stick his hand in and get one? You?

MAGICIAN: *(Interrupting)*: Hey! Hey! Santa Claus doesn't give out stuff like that!

SANTA: Look buddy, the gnomes are on strike, the Fisher Price consignment's stuck at customs, I have to take what I can get. Go sort out your own problems. *(To someone in the audience)*: Nice jellyfish?

SECOND SIDEKICK: We think you're an imposter. *(To the audience)*: Don't we?

SANTA: Oh that's very good, isn't it? I spend all year slaving, with no one to talk to but elves and trolls, and when I come down to hand out the seafood you say I'm a fake. Very polite. Well let me tell you there's only two fellas living at the North Pole, and you wouldn't catch Superman putting jellyfish down anyone's socks. I am Santa Claus!

FIRST SIDEKICK: *(Rallying the audience)*: Oh no you're not!

SANTA: Oh yes I am!

ALL BUT SANTA: Oh no you're not!

SANTA: Oh yes I am!

ALL BUT SANTA: Oh no you're not!

SANTA: Oh yes I am, and I can prove it! Here . . . *(He produces a lump of red plasticine or some similar object)*: Rudolf's nose!

ALL BUT SANTA: *(withdrawing in shock)*: Rudolf's nose?

SANTA: We use it for lighting in the dark room.

MAGICIAN: What happened to Rudolf?

SANTA: Tragedy. Patch of black ice on top of the World Trade Building. But that's another story. Does this, or does this not, prove that I am Santa?

ALL BUT SANTA: *(After conferring)*: Yes.

SANTA: So what are you staring at?

MAGICIAN: We . . . we just thought you'd be *different*.

SANTA: Rosy cheeks, red suit, three billion chimneys in one night? C'mon! That's just rumours.

MAGICIAN: But *jellyfish* . . . !

SANTA: Well it's not all jellyfish. I do have one other present . . . *(He hands a small wrapped present to the child)*

MAGICIAN: What's that?

SANTA: *(With a glance at the audience)*: A seaslug!

(Immediately, the MAGICIAN and SIDEKICKS line up with SANTA and join in the song)

EVERYONE:

Oh, you'd better watch out,
You'd better not cry,
You'd better not pout –
I'm telling you why . . .
Santa Claus is coming to town,
(Bu-jeebu-doobu, bu-jeebu-doo-du!)

(The performers go into the audience handing out small presents – 'seaslugs' – to the children)

Radio Religion

Characters: 3 principals, at least 3 others
Performance time: 3 minutes

I sometimes wonder what it would be like if the kind of religious people who have absolutely no interest in attracting mass support for their views got together and opened a radio station. If they did, there might be a demand for programmes like BLUMBOLDT's 'Snuff it'. The sketch mimics the bland, tumbling commercial sound familiar to anyone who has tried to doze off on the beach at Blackpool. Making it work depends chiefly on two things: one, ensuring that all the characters speak with intense animation; and two, keeping the pace rattling along so there's never more than half a second of silence unless the script requires it. As for the jingles, feel free to improvise.

(At the start of the sketch the CONTESTANT is off. All the characters on stage assume the pose of announcers on a vintage radio show – hand over ear – forming two groups around real or imaginary stand-up mikes. BLUMBOLDT and TEASER are to stage left; the rest, forming the JINGLE, to stage right. Central in the JINGLE is the DIRECTOR, who conducts the sound effects. Further to stage right lies a

table with a telephone on top. A short silence precedes the DIRECTOR's cue)

DIRECTOR; *(Counting the seconds with strokes of his arm)*: Okay. Quiet. Three, two, one – *on air.*

JINGLE: *(As a clock)*: Dum . . . dum . . . dum . . .

BLUMBOLDT: Three o'clock in the afternoon and you're tuned in to:

JINGLE: *(Singing)*: Holy holy holy – Radio Religion!

BLUMBOLDT: Yes indeed. This is Harry Blumboldt hosting another edition of

JINGLE: *Snuff it!*

BLUMBOLDT: – the radio quiz that tests your knowledge of tradition, tradition, tradition and tradition – all that matters to the *seriously religious* person. With me as usual is Dr Mildred Teaser, Calvinist envoy to the Vatican and agony aunt for the *Church Times*

JINGLE: *(Singing)*: It's Marvellous Marvellous Marvellous Mildred!

TEASER: Hello, Harry, it's great to be here. And first off a big, big thank you to all of you who wrote in for this week's Outstanding Achievement Award. The winner –

JINGLE: Yes?

TEASER: is

JINGLE: *Yes?*

TEASER: Euphemia Birdshot of Greenock, who hasn't cracked a smile for twenty-five years.

JINGLE: *(Whoops and applause)*

TEASER: Isn't that tremendous? Congratulations, Daphne. A 50 pence book token is on its way to you, exchangable in the Turkish History department of any popular bookshop.

JINGLE: *(Singing)*: Allelu – ia!

BLUMBOLDT: Yes, well done, Daphne, and the rest of you – keep those postcards coming in. Okay. Later on in the show we'll be looking at a new book on serious religion, called *Bored Again*; and we'll also be telling you at which British church you can hear noises like *these* –

JINGLE: *(A sharp, 2 second blast of hysterical babbling and sealion impersonations)*

TEASER: – and why *you* shouldn't go there. All this and more coming your way on:

JINGLE: *(Singing)*: Holy holy holy – Radio Religion! Plays the game!

BLUMBOLDT: But we kick off with our telephone quiz. You know the rules. We light three candles; you have to snuff them out by answering questions correctly. Get one wrong, you burn your fingers and we press the *Ow!* button –

JINGLE: *Ow!*

(Here the CONTESTANT appears, from off stage or out of the crowd, to sit on

the edge of the table. He wears a stylish suit and sunglasses)

TEASER: – get one right, and you could be on your way to a luxury weekend for two in a Trappist monastery. So get on that line!

JINGLE: Will they win or will they fluff it? Find out soon as we play – *Snuff it!*

(The CONTESTANT picks up the telephone)

JINGLE: *Brrr Brrr! Brrr Brrr!*

BLUMBOLDT: Our first contestant today is someone who obviously takes his religion very seriously indeed – are you there, God . . . ?

CONTESTANT: *(Dazzling)*: Sure am, Harry. Always was and always will be, Alpha and Omega, the voice divine on the telephone line!

BLUMBOLDT: Oho! a *headcase*!

CONTESTANT: You got it. Head of the case, treble to bass. B'*dahm* – b'*dicha*doo*bahm* – b'*dichadicha*doom . . . !

BLUMBOLDT: And what do you do, God?

CONTESTANT: What do I *do*?

BLUMBOLDT: As a job, from nine to five;

CONTESTANT: Nine to five, midnight to midnight, noon till noon I call new worlds into bein' and stick fallen stars back in the firmament. You could call me the managin' director of the universe.

BLUMBOLDT: Of course. What else? The man's called God, he runs the universe.

CONTESTANT: With a new occupation on the radio station. In short, Harry, I run *you*!

BLUMBOLDT: *(No taking this seriously)*: You don't!

CONTESTANT: True as blue, I do, Harry.

BLUMBOLDT: *(Laughing lightly)*: Well, we get all kinds on this show. If you're ready for your first question, God, we'll go over to Mildred . . .

JINGLE: *(Singing)*: It's Marvellous Marvellous Marvellous Mildred!

CONTESTANT: Fly it by me, Millie babe.

TEASER: Question number one: what instruments is it proper to use in church?

CONTESTANT: Whoo! Tubas, trombones, saxophones; tambourines and drum machines – whatever gives *you* the *kick*!

JINGLE: *Ow!*

CONTESTANT: As I thought! A one track mind of the keyboard kind: the organ.

BLUMBOLDT: The whole organ, and nothing but the organ. A tough starter, God. On to question two.

TEASER: Wearing Levis on Sunday gives you eczema behind the knees – true or false?

CONTESTANT: False.

JINGLE: *Ow!*

BLUMBOLDT: True.

CONTESTANT: False.

JINGLE: *Ow!*

BLUMBOLDT: True.

CONTESTANT: Partners please for the false waltz. The biggest bore on the dance floor . . .

BLUMBOLDT: I'm sorry, the judge's decision is final. God, that leaves you one more chance to snuff it.

CONTESTANT: More than I can say for you, Harry.

(As TEASER speaks, the CONTESTANT firmly replaces the handset and stands up. Facing away from BLUMBOLDT he reaches into his pocket and thoughtfully unwraps a large cigar)

TEASER: Question number three: who or what did Moses call a whitewashed sepulchre? Was it: (a) the South African Government; (b) the Pentagon; or (c) the ghost of Hamlet's father?

JINGLE: *(Almost immediately, one tick per second)*: Tick, tick, tick, tick, tick, tick . . .

BLUMBOLDT: *(Voice-over the JINGLE's ticking)*: I'm afraid we're going to have to put the clock on you for this one . . .

JINGLE: PING!

BLUMBOLDT: It was of course a trick question. Moses never used the phrase at all, it was St Augustine. Well, God, I'm sorry to say you've missed out on that fun holiday weekend. But since you were such a great contestant we'll be sending you a compilation album of the world's slowest hymn tunes, and your own personalized *I've snuffed it* sticker . . . .

(Towards the end of BLUMBOLDT's last speech the CONTESTANT decisively turns to face the audience, removes the cigar, and again picks up the handset)

CONTESTANT: Put me through to head office. I wanna brief with the chief.

TEASER: You're tuned in to:

JINGLE: *(Singing)*: Holy holy holy – Radio Religion!

CONTESTANT: Hey, Fritz the pitz. The coolest joe on the radio! Been a long time!

BLUMBOLDT: Join us again in just a couple of minutes for Round Two.

CONTESTANT: Now, Fritz, I wanna word about this goonball game show . . .

TEASER: Don't go away. Remember you're listening to the *serious* station.

CONTESTANT: You got it, Fritz. Forget the profit. Get it off the air, right now.

JINGLE: Will they win or will they fluff it? Find out soon as we –

CONTESTANT: Yes!

EVERYONE ELSE: *OW!*

(The last two lines complete the metre and must maintain the rhythm. Precisely in time with the OW! *two things happen: the CONTESTANT slaps the handset back on the holder, and then JINGLE, BLUMBOLDT and TEASER all turn their heads sharply in his direction. All freeze)*

Boating for Gophers (The Four Part Flood Rap)

Characters: 4
Performance time: 2 minutes

A few words are in order about the notation used below. Each set of parts (soprano, alto, tenor, bass) covers two bars in 4/4 time. The beats are numbered, and any word or syllable whose first letter is directly under a number is spoken on that beat. Look at the bass line from the eighth set:

```
        1       3      3        4       1      2       3      4
(B)     *       I need some one to      do a    job    for     me.
```

The symbol '' on beat 1 marks a single handclap. The first seven syllables are quavers, 'need', 'one' and 'do' falling on the beat, 'job' and 'me' are crotchets, 'for' is also a crotchet, but is syncopated, in other words spoken just before the beat so as to spring the rhythm. Syncopations occur throughout and are indicated by the printing of a syllable slightly to the left of its beat number. The double handclaps found elsewhere are equivalent to a pair of quavers and can be of two kinds: '**', where the beat is on the first clap, and '* – *', where it's on the second.*

All rapping leans heavily on the performers' sense of rhythm, and on their ability to bring the sound to life. BOATING FOR GOPHERS makes the additional demand that the lead line be swapped rapidly, sometimes several times in succession, as the tenor's narration is cut into by the bass (as God) and by the alto (as Noah). If you don't want to go crazy, start by taking it slow.

	1	2	3	4	1	2	3	4
(S)								
(A)								
(T)	One		two,		a-one,	two	three,	well

(B)	1	2	3	4	1	2	3	4
(S)				Very!				
(A)				Very!				
(T)	once up-	on a	time,	a	long	time a-	go,	the
				Very!				

	1	2	3	4	1	2	3	4
(S)						Oh	no!	Just
(A)						Oh	no!	Just
(T)	Lord	saw the	people	and he	said:	Oh	no!	Just
(B)						Oh	no!	Just

	1	2	3	4	1	2	3	4
(S)	look!				I	in-	tend,	
(A)	look!				I	in-	tend,	
(T)	look!				I	in-	tend,	
(B)	look	wha'the'r	doin',	not as	I	in-	tend,	Think I'll

	1	2	3	4	1	2	3	4
(S)	*	Oh,	oh,	oh!	Over	a-	gain.	
(A)	*	Oh,	oh,	oh!	Over	a-	gain.	
(T)	*	Oh,	oh,	oh!	Over	a-	gain.	
(B)	*wipe the	slate	clean and	start	over	a-	gain.	And I

	1	2	3	4	1	2	3	4
(S)		Yes, he	means it,					
(A)		Yes, he	means it,					
(T)		Yes, he	means it,					So he
(B)	mean it.			So you'd	better	watch	out!	

	1	2	3	4	1	2	3	4
(S)		Hey!		a-	*Boom!	*Bang!	*Boom!	
(A)		Hey!		a-	*Boom!	*Bang!	*Boom!	
(T)	called	up the	thunder	clouds:	*one,	*two,	*three!	And he
(B)		Hey!		a-	*Boom!	*Bang!	*Boom!	

	1	2	3	4	1	2	3	4
(S)								Sir!
(A)								Sir!
(T)	said:							Sir!
(B)		I need some one to		do a	job	for	me.	

	1	2	3	4	1	2	3	4
(S)		Gather,		water,	oppor-	tune	time	then
(A)		Gather,		water,	oppor-	tune	time	then
(T)		Gather,		water,	oppor-	tune	time	then
(B)	Gather	all the	water	for the	oppor-	tune	time	then

	1	2	3	4	1	2	3	4
(S)	wait,							
(A)	wait,							
(T)	wait,							
(B)	wait	while I	wake up	an old	friend	of	mine.	Hey,

	1	2	3	4	1	2	3	4
(S)		Tick,		tick,		tick,		tick,
(A)		Tick,		tick,		tick,		tick.
(T)			Tock,		tock,		tock.	
(B)	Noah!							Oh,

	1	2	3	4	1	2	3	4
(S)		Tick,		tick,	ringa-	dinga-	ringa	dinga!
(A)		Tick,		tick, a-	beeeeeeeeeeeeeeeeeeeeeeeeeeeeeeeeep!			
(T)	Noah!!		Cuckoo!		Cuckoo!	Cuck!	Cuck!	Cuck!
(B)	Noah!!							

	1	2	3	4	1	2	3	4
(S)	Rise	and	shine,		rise	and	shine,	
(A)				What?		O-	kay!	
(T)		he	said,					
(B)	Noah,				Noah!		You'd	better

	1	2	3	4	1	2	3	4
(S)	bend	and	stretch	and	rise	and	shine.	Huh!
(A)								Huh!
(T)								Huh!
(B)	get up	off your	bed be-	fore I	wash it	a-	way!	Huh!

	1	2	3	4	1	2	3	4
(S)	Rise	and	shine,		rise	and	shine,	
(A)	Rise	and	shine,		rise	and	shine,	
(T)								
(B)	Round up	all the	people	that you	think are	any	good,	and

	1	2	3	4	1	2	3	4
(S)	yawn,		yawn,		yawn,		yawn.	
(A)								What?
(T)	yawn,		yawn,		yawn,		yawn,	
(B)	put them	in an	ark	made of	go-	pher	wood.	

	1	2	3	4	1	2	3	4
(S)	Go-	pher	wood!					Oh,
(A)								Oh,
(T)	Go-	pher	wood!					Oh,
(B)	Go-	pher	wood! Y'	know, dem	little	furry	things?	

	1	2	3	4	1	2	3	4
(S)	doze!		Three,		two,		one,	
(A)	doze	little	furry	things!	Coming	right	up,	God!
(T)	doze!							
(B)								

	1	2	3	4	1	2	3	4
(S)					Yik	yak,	tik	tak!
(A)					Yik	yak,	tik	tak!
(T)	a-rooba	dooba	dik	dak, a-	rooba	dooba	dooba	dik!
(B)	a-rooba	dooba	dik	dak, a-	rooba	dooba	dooba	dik!

	1	2	3	4	1	2	3	4
(S)	Bzzzzzzzzzzzzzzzzzzzzzzzzzzzzzzzzz!				Bik	BIK-bik	BIK-bik	BIK-bik!
(A)			Yow!		Yow!	Yow!	Yow!	Yow!
(T)	a-dum!	Hammer!		Hammer!	a-	rooba	deeby	doob!
(B)	a-dum!	Hammer!		Hammer!	a-	rooba	deeby	doob!

	1	2	3	4	1	2	3	4
(S)				Clit	clat,	clit	clat	clit!
(A)				Clit	clat,	clit	clat	clit!
(T) a-	rooba	dooba	dik	dak, a-	rooba	dooba	dooba	dik!
(B) a-	rooba	dooba	dik	dak, a-	rooba	dooba	dooba	dik!

	1	2	3	4	1	2	3	4
(S)	Yimmer	yammer,	yimmer	yammer!				Phew!
(A)			Yow!		Yabba	dabba	do!	Phew!
(T) a-	dum!	Hammer!		Hammer!				Phew!
(B) a-	dum!	Hammer!		Hammer!				Phew!

	1	2	3	4	1	2	3	4
(S)				*				
(A)				*				
(T)		said God,		*				
(B)	Noah,			That's a	mighty	fine	boat,	And

	1	2	3	4	1	2	3	4
(S)								*Yeah!
(A)								*Yeah!
(T)								*Yeah!
(B)	any	time now	I'm	gonna	see if	it'll	float.	*Yeah! So,

	1	2	3	4	1	2	3	4
(S)					two	by	two,	
(A)					two	by	two,	
(T)					two	by	two,	
(B)	bring	down the	ani-	mals a-	two	by	two	and

	1	2	3	4	1	2	3	4
(S)Re-	member,					Rabbit,	rabbit,	rabbit!
(A)Re-	member,					Rabbit,	rabbit,	rabbit!
(T)Re-	member,				sepa-	rate	rooms.	
(B)Re-	member:	put the	rabbits	in	sepa-	rate	rooms.	I want

	1	2	3	4	1	2	3	4
(S)	Left,	right,	left,	right,	left,	right,	left,	yuk!
(A)	Left,	right,	left,	right,	left,	right,	left,	yuk!
(T)			musk	rats,			toads?	
(B)	alli-	gators,			ele-	phants and	. . .	that's it!

	1	2	3	4	1	2	3	4
(S)		Quick,	speed it	up, and	every	kind of	what d'y	call it?
(A)		Quick,	speed it	up, and	every	kind of	what d'y	call it?
(T)	Every	kind of	creepy	crawley.				
(B)					Every	kind of	what d'y	call it?

	1	2	3	4	1	2	3	4
(S)							snorters,	
(A)						squeakers,		
(T)	Great big	purple	people	eaters,				bleaters.
(B)					barkers,			

	1	2	3	4	1	2	3	4
(S)	Ants!			fleas,	spiders,	vultures,	ducks.	
(A)	Ants!	bugs,			spiders,	vultures,	ducks.	
(T)	Ants!				spiders,	vultures,	ducks.	
(B)	Ants!		mice,		spiders,	vultures,	ducks, and	please,

	1	2	3	4	1	2	3	4
(S)				*				
(A)		Yes,	God?	*				
(T)				*				
(B)	Noah . . .			*	Don't	for-get the	goph-	ers!

	1	2	3	4	1	2	3	4
(S)	**		**		**		**	
(A)	**		**		**		**	
(T)	**		**		**	Then	God	said:
(B)	**		**		**		**	

	1	2	3	4	1	2	3	4
(S)				a-rabba	doomba	bam	boom!	*
(A)				a-rabba	doomba	bam	boom!	*
(T)				a-rabba	doomba	bam	boom!	*
(B)	Bring o-	n the	thunder!					*And

	1	2	3	4	1	2	3	4
(S)				a-rabba	doomba	bam	boom!	*
(A)				a-rabba	doomba	bam	boom!	*
(T)				a-rabba	doomba	bam	boom!	*
(B)	bring o-	n the	rain!					*And

	1	2	3	4	1	2	3	4
(S)				a-rabba	doomba	bam	boom!	*
(A)				a-rabba	doomba	bam	boom!	*
(T)				a-rabba	doomba	bam	boom!	*
(B)	bring o-	n the	wind!					*And

	1	2	3	4	1	2	3	4
(S)				*				*
(A)				*				*
(T)				*	Bring o-	n the	flood!	*
(B)	bring o-	n the	flood.	*	Bring o-	n the	flood!	*

	1	2	3	4	1	2	3	4
(S)				*	Bring o-	n the	flood!	A-
(A)	Bring o-	n the	flood!	*	Bring o-	n the	flood!	
(T)	Bring o-	n the	flood!	*	Bring o-	n the	flood!	A-
(B)	bring o-	n the	flood.	*	Bring o-	n the	flood!	A-

	1	2	3	4	1	2	3	4
(S)	r-		ub a-	dub	dub!			A-
(A)	My	gosh it's	raining,	pouring,	listen	to that	gale	warning,
(T)	r-		ub a-	dub	dub!			A-
(B)	r-		ub a-	dub	dub!			A-

	1	2	3	4	1	2	3	4
(S)	r-		ub a-	dub	dub!			A-
(A)	boy, I'm	scared and	that's the	truth, I	hope those	workmen	fixed the	roof,
(T)	r-		ub a-	dub	dub:			A-
(B)	r-		ub a-	dub	dub!			A-

	1	2	3	4	1	2	3	4
(S)	r-		ub a-	dub	dub!			A-
(A)	re-member,	Noah,	feed the	cats and	walk the	dogs and	chase the	rats, and
(T)	r-		ub a-	dub	dub!			A-
(B)	r-		ub a-	dub	dub!			A-

	1	2	3	4	1	2	3	4
(S)	r-		ub a-	dub,			sea	sick!
(A)	Noah,	here's the	real	trick –	don't	get	sea	sick!
(T)	r-		ub a-	dub,			sea	sick!
(B)	r-		ub a-	dub,			sea	sick!

	1	2	3	4	1	2	3	4
(S)	One	* h-	undred	*and	twen-	*ty	days *-	* the
(A)	One	* h-	undred	*and	twen-	*ty	days *-	* the
(T)	One	* h-	undred	*and	twen-	*ty	days *-	* the
(B)	One	* h-	undred	*and	twen-	*ty	days *-	* the

	1	2	3	4	1	2	3	4
(S)	ark	*	rocked u-	*pon the	rol-	*ling	waves. *-	* The
(A)	ark	*	rocked u-	*pon the	rol-	*ling	waves. *-	* The
(T)	ark	*	rocked u-	*pon the	rol-	*ling	waves. *-	* The
(B)	ark	*	rocked u-	*pon the	rol-	*ling	waves. *-	* The

	1	2	3	4	1	2	3	4
(S)	sun	*was	darkened	*and the	tem-	*pest	raged *-	* for
(A)	sun	*was	darkened	*and the	tem-	*pest	raged *-	* for
(T)	sun	*was	darkened	*and the	tem-	*pest	raged *-	* for
(B)	sun	*was	darkened	*and the	tem-	*pest	raged *-	* for

	1	2	3	4	1	2	3	4
(S)	one	* h-	undred	*and	twen-	*ty	days. And	then:
(A)	one	* h-	undred	*and	twen-	*ty	days. And	then:
(T)	one	* h-	undred	*and	twen-	*ty	days. And	then:
(B)	one	* h-	undred	*and	twen-	*ty	days. And	then.

	1	2	3	4	1	2	3	4
(S)	Bump!		Bump!	**				
(A)	Bump!		Bump!	**				
(T)	Bump!		Bump!	**				Well,
(B)	Bump!		Bump!	**		All	change!	

	1	2	3	4	1	2	3	4
(S)							and	let out
(A)	Noah	knew he'd	landed	so he	opened	up the	zoo and	let out
(T)							and	let out
(B)							and	let out

	1	2	3	4	1	2	3	4
(S)	*			Rabbit,		rabbit,		rabbit,
(A)	*				rabbit,		rabbit,	
(T)	* five	thousand	rabbits	and a	gopher	or two,		
(B)	*							Oh, and

	1	2	3	4	1	2	3	4
(S)								
(A)								
(T)		said God,						
(B)	Noah,		you've	got your	feet back	on the	ground,	but

	1	2	3	4	1	2	3	4
(S)	Be careful				Monkey-	ing a-	round!	No
(A)	Be careful!				Monkey-	ing a-	round!	No
(T)	Be careful!				Monkey-	ing a-	round!	No
(B)	Be careful –	I don't	want to	see no	monkey-	ing a-	round!	No

	1	2	3	4	1	2	3	4
(S)	way!							Yeah?
(A)	way!							Yeah?
(T)	way! So	if you're	looking	for a	moral	in this	tale,	it's
(B)	way!							Yeah?

	1	2	3	4	1	2	3	4
(S)		Lay it	on me,	brother!				
(A)		Lay it	on me,	brother!				
(T)	this:				If you	would pre-	vail	you must
(B)		Lay it	on me,	brother!				

	1	2	3	4	1	2	3	4
(S)		Halle-	lujah!					
(A)		Halle-	lujah!					
(T)	learn to			do what	any	gopher	would, and	go for
(B)		Halle-	lujah!					

	1	2	3	4	1	2	3	4
(S)		*		*		*		*
(A)		*		*		*		*
(T)	hope	*in	God, or	*y'll be	gone	*for	good. And	*go for
(B)		*		*			And	*go for

	1	2	3	4	1	2	3	4
(S)		*		*	Gone	*for	good	*go
(A)		*		*	Gone	*for	good	*go
(T)	hope	*in	God, or	*y'll be	gone	*for	good, And	*go for
(B)	hope	*in	God, or	*y'll be	gone	*for	good, And	*go for

	1	2	3	4	1	2	3	4
(S)	hope	*in	God or	*y'll be	gone	*gone	*gon*-o gon	-*o* gone.
(A)	hope	*in	God, or	*y'll be	gone	*gone	*gon*-o gon	-*o* gone.
(T)	hope,	*yeah . . .		*		*gone	*gon*-o gon	-*o* gone.
(B)	hope	*in	God, or	*y'll be	gone	*gone	*gon*-o gon	-*o* gone

	1	2	3	4	1	2	3	4
(S)	Hope,	*ooh, in	God,	*ooh, or	gone	*for	good.	*Dat's
(A)	Hope,	*ooh, in	God,	*ooh, or	gone	*for	good.	*Dat's
(T)	Hope in	*God,	ah,	*ooh, or	gone	*for	good.	*Dat's
(B)	Hope,	*ooh,	ah, in	*God, or	gone	*for	good.	*Dat's

	1	2	3	4	1	2	3	4
(S)	de' end of	de	rap.	Hope y've	un	der	stood!	
(A)	de' end of	de	rap.	Hope y've	un	der	stood!	
(T)	de' end of	de	rap.	Hope y've	un	der	stood!	
(B)	de' end of	de	rap.	Hope y've	un	der	stood!	(Hey,

	1	2	3	4	1	2	3	4
(S)								
(A)								
(T)								

(B) Noah, how many rabbits did you put in there . . .?)

Rattlers

Characters: 2 principals, at least 8 others
Performance time: 2 minutes

Ezekiel's vision of the dry bones takes well to children's drama. This version of the story requires little memorization, and so can be done at short notice in the classroom if you're willing to improvise the props. Sound effects are essential. Each of the BONES will need a pair of 'rattlers' – small objects that make a good noise when struck together. Practically anything will do – wooden blocks, pebbles, spoons and tin cups; the wider the range, the better the sound. Prudent, though, not to take risks with your grandmother's china.

(EZEKIEL and the READER stand stage right; the BONES, grouped closely, with the SKY and the WINDS behind, to stage left. Out of sight of the audience the SKY is holding an image of the sun mounted on a short stick; each of the four WINDS has a silk scarf. All the BONES carry rattlers)

READER: Ezekiel was a prophet.

EZEKIEL: God's prophet.

READER: And God gave him dreams.

EZEKIEL: Visions.

READER: Messages.

EZEKIEL: God's messages.

READER: And Ezekiel would write them down in his book, for everyone to read . . .

EZEKIEL: One day the Lord took me to the desert . . .

(On the word 'desert' the SKY makes the sun rise by slowly swinging it up to the vertical. The WINDS, standing to either side of the SKY, raise their scarves to different heights, holding them by the two top corners to suggest a scattering of small clouds. The BONES subside until they are lying motionless on the floor)

READER: The sky was blue. The sun was hot.

EZEKIEL: And the desert was covered in bones.

READER: As white as china!

EZEKIEL: Bone dry!

READER: And God said: Ezekiel, can these bones live?

EZEKIEL: Lord, only *you* know that.

READER: Speak to these bones, Ezekiel. Say to them: Dry bones, hear the word of the Lord!

(At this the BONES sit up)

I will join you together. I will cover you with flesh.

EZEKIEL: Then I heard a rattling sound!

(The BONES begin to rattle)

READER: The bones came together!

EZEKIEL: Bodies grew! All wrapped up in skin!

(EZEKIEL raises his hand as a signal to the BONES. Abruptly they stop rattling)

READER: But they weren't alive.

EZEKIEL: They weren't breathing.

READER: So God said: Come from the four winds, O breath.

EZEKIEL: Come to this desert.

READER: And make these people live!

(On the word 'live' the BONES again begin to rattle. The WINDS move out and, trailing their scarves in the air, run two circuits around the BONES before returning to their original position, their hands at their sides. As the winds run, the BONES stand up and the SKY makes the sun set. EZEKIEL then raises his hand a second time. The BONES stop rattling)

EZEKIEL:	And the bones stood up – a vast army of living people!
READER:	A spooky story!
EZEKIEL:	A message.
READER:	But a message for who?
BONES:	For us!
EZEKIEL:	Dry bones.
READER:	Lonely.
EZEKIEL:	Sad.
READER:	Broken.
EZEKIEL:	God brings us together.
READER:	Makes us well.
EZEKIEL:	Breathes in his Spirit.
READER:	Gives us:
EVERYONE:	*(Thrusting both hands into the air)*: Life!

Not a Nudist Club

Characters: 2
Performance time: 2 minutes

A human being will react in one of two ways to what Christianity calls sin: he will feel guilty, or he will not feel guilty. The first is assumed by the writer of Genesis in the story of the Fall; the second – which if less appropriate is equally human – provides the basis of the following sketch. Thinking that GOD's attention is diverted ADAM employs his new-found knowledge and assumes the role of the urban sophisticate. GOD (whose voice is presented to best effect with the help of a PA system) has of course known what the score is from the start. But the Creator decides to wait a while before making that call . . .

(Front centre stage is a small table with a telephone. It rings, and in a moment ADAM appears, wearing a leotard and a very large fig leaf. He is obviously in high spirits. He polishes the apple he is carrying, and takes a bite from it before lifting the handset. The ringing ceases)

ADAM: Eden one one one, one one one one. Adam speaking.

GOD: Good afternoon, Adam.

ADAM. Oh – hi, God. Haven't heard from you for a while.

GOD: No – I thought you and Eve might like a little time to yourselves. How are you getting along?

ADAM: Great. Absolutely great. Got to hand it to you, God. It's a marriage made in heaven.

GOD: Yes . . . Adam, I wonder if you can help me?

ADAM: Sure thing.

GOD: I have reason to believe a serpent's been let loose in the garden.

ADAM: *(Taking another bite)*: Give me a description?

GOD: It's long and slimy.

ADAM: That's all right, I can handle it.

GOD: The *serpent* is long and slimy.

ADAM: Oh, right, I've got you – it's kind of a cross between a worm and an alligator and it goes around telling people to eat the forbidden fruit?

GOD: Yes.

ADAM: No. Never laid eyes on it.

GOD: You're sure?

ADAM: Sure as birds have beaks, God. What's the problem?

GOD: Well, the thing is, Adam, there's an apple missing off the tree of the knowledge of good and evil.

ADAM: What? No! Missing? An apple! Horrors!

GOD: So if you've seen anything suspicious . . .

ADAM: *(Contemplating the apple)*: No . . . no . . . can't put my finger on anything. *(He takes another bite)*

GOD: Oh well, it was just on the off chance. Next time you're in the orchard keep your eyes peeled. Okay?

ADAM: Long and slimy?

GOD: Long and slimy.

ADAM: I'll watch out for it. Well, must fly. It's nice talking to you, God. Anything else?

GOD: Just one thing –

ADAM: Sure.

GOD: Why are you wearing that fig leaf?

(Adam chokes and fumbles the apple into his leotard. He looks at the handset, then around the stage)

ADAM: I thought it might be, ah, . . . I mean you don't want the place turning into a nudist club . . .

GOD: A nudist club, Adam?

ADAM: Well . . . you know . . . a place where, ah . . .

GOD: Yes?

ADAM: A place where people take their clothes off.

GOD: I don't remember people having clothes *on* in the first place.

ADAM: No. No, well . . . let's talk about it tomorrow, God. Okay? Love to Gabriel and the crew. Bye!

(He puts the handset down, leans on the table and mops his brow)

GOD: I want to talk about it now, Adam!

(ADAM jumps, and clutches his heart)

ADAM: You can't do that! I just hung up on you!

GOD: You're lucky I haven't hung up on *you*. Now, I think there's something you should tell me . . .

ADAM: I'm clean, God. Really, I'm clean.

GOD: Then what do you understand by the word 'evil', Adam?

ADAM: Well, evil is . . . it depends. I mean, do you want evil as defined by Plato, Aristotle, Aquinas, Calvin, Kant, Hegel, Marx, Barth, Tillich, Sartre – ?

GOD: Adam!

ADAM: – all right. It was me.

GOD: You took the apple.

ADAM: Yes.

GOD: The apple I specifically told you not to take.

ADAM: Yes.

GOD: And because you realized you had no clothes on you dressed up in that ridiculous fig leaf?

ADAM: Yes.

GOD: Why did you do it, Adam?

ADAM: Well, God, you've got to be fair. *(He spreads his hands out wide in an appealing gesture)*: I mean, *everybody's doing it!*

Pigg

Characters: 3
Performance time: 4 minutes

'What does a woman want?' asked Freud. Like most men, he didn't know. But he did at least try to find out, which is more than you can say for the likes of Tyrone PIGG. PIGG is the ubiquitous chat show host, urbane, talkative, but fronting a programme that exists solely to massage the male ego. If he appears gross (and he may be a little too gross for some church congregations), it is only to make the point that human beings all too readily trespass on one another's freedom. The atmosphere of the TV show is more effectively suggested if people are planted in the audience to encourage applause. The PRESENTER can be played by CRUTNEY.

(There are two chairs centre stage, separated by a low coffee table on which stands a vase of flowers. Above and behind the furniture, mounted in large letters, is the word. ***Pigg****)*

PRESENTER: *(A voice off, with gusto)*: And now, a big hand please for your host this evening, Tyrone Caesar Pigg!

(PIGG runs on stage, grinning and waving down the applause. He stands in front of the furniture)

PIGG: Thank you! Thank you! Good evening, and welcome once again to television's only chauvenist chat show. You know, countless times men have stopped me on the street and said, 'Tyrone, show me the perfect woman. Show me the perfect woman because my wife – she won't cook, she won't clean the house, she won't, you know, wear that pink snakeskin lingerie that cost me two hundred guineas in Harrods . . . Show me the perfect woman!' Well, tonight I am going to do just that. Will you please welcome the most talked about man of the year, the inventor of the brand new *designer* female, Aussie to beat all Aussies – Malcolm Crutney!

(PIGG leads applause as CRUTNEY enters, they shake hands and sit down)

PIGG: Malcolm, I understand your designer woman's already a sell-out in Australia.

CRUTNEY: Yeah, it's goin' like the proverbial bushfire down under, Tyrone. B'lieve in the last seven days we've sold more women than stuffed koalas.

PIGG: You're launching it in Britain this week. How much is the designer woman going to cost?

CRUTNEY: Twenty-five thousand big ones, and if we like you we throw in a can of XXXX.

PIGG: A good buy?

CRUTNEY: You betcha life. Does the housecleaning in thirty seconds, and if y'wanna have the boys round for a beer after the game y'just stick her in the cupboard.

PIGG: *(To the audience)*: Isn't that something! *(To CRUTNEY)* Now, Malcolm, you've kindly agreed to bring one of your models here and put her through her paces. Would you like to introduce her to us?

CRUTNEY: Be delighted, Mr Pigg.

(They both stand)

PIGG: *(To the audience)*: Gentlemen, in a television exclusive, we bring you Malcolm Crutney's designer woman!

(They move in front of the furniture, applauding her as she comes on. SHEILA, in evening dress and carrying a clutch bag, enters like a model on a catwalk, and stands between them in a shop-window pose, centre stage, looking forward, expressionless)

(Admiring her): Oh – la belle femme! And this is the first designer woman you ever produced?

CRUTNEY: Yeah, this model's called The Sheila. After my dog.

(PIGG takes SHEILA's hand and presses it to his lips)

PIGG: Good evening . . . Sheila.

BRENDA: *(Unctiously, but without shifting her gaze)*: Good evening . . . Tyrone.

PIGG: *(Releasing her hand. To the audience)*: Oh, ho ho! Isn't that something! *(To CRUTNEY)*: Would I be right in saying she has some sort of brain in there?

CRUTNEY: Yeah, it's ackch'ly a standard female brain. We tinkered about with it, of course. Took out the bit that makes decisions and filled up on extra beauty tips and past issues of *Vogue*. Saves Sheila having to think too much. Pretty humane, really.

PIGG: So in effect she's a slave to the male ego.

CRUTNEY: Yeah. Sublime, isn't it? Wanna see a demonstration?

PIGG: Sure.

CRUTNEY: Sheila – kiss him!

BRENDA: *(Throwing herself on PIGG)*: Oh, darling, darling!

CRUTNEY: Now kiss him in French.

BRENDA: Oh, mon chou, mon chou!

CRUTNEY: Heel!

(SHEILA abruptly resumes her former position, leaving

PIGG to blow out his cheeks and straighten his tie)

You see, Mr Pigg, Sheila underwent what we call the 'garden test'. We put her in a garden of fruit trees – peaches, mangoes, the lot. We said to her, 'You can eat any fruit you like, 'cept the apples on that big one in the middle. Eat *them*, and you'll turn from a mindless automation into a free human being. And by the way, the apple's the only fruit under twenty-five calories – the rest'll make you blow up like a Zeppelin!'

PIGG: And she didn't eat it?

CRUTNEY: Didn't even look. Sheila does exactly what she's told. *(He pats her bottom)*: don't you sweetheart? You can even trust her with money.

PIGG: No!

CRUTNEY: Give her your credit card.

PIGG: *(With a grin at the audience – the parrying is deliberate)*: My credit card!

CRUTNEY: Go on. Give it to her. She won't use it.

PIGG: Okay. The big test!

(He gives SHEILA the card, which she holds in her fingertips)

(To the audience): Isn't that something!

(Suddenly both PIGG and CRUTNEY freeze.

SHEILA opens her clutch bag, drops the credit card inside, and proceeds to check her lipstick in a small hand mirror. She winks at the audience as she puts this away and resumes the shop-window pose. As she freezes, PIGG and CRUTNEY unfreeze)

'Tyrone, show me the perfect woman.' If any of you are saying that tonight, say it no more! Because tonight, right here in the studio, we are putting Sheila up for auction! The money goes to this month's charity – *Playboy Magazine*; the credit goes to Crutney Enterprise International; the designer woman goes to you. You like that?

(PIGG, CRUTNEY and collaborators stir up a round of applause and a few whoops)

Malcolm, would you like to name the starting price?

CRUTNEY: The starting price is: thirty thousand pounds.

PIGG: And here we go! Who's going to get the ball rolling with thirty thousand? Over there? Yes – thank you, sir. Now, thirty-five thousand? Thirty-five thousand in the middle, thank you. Forty thousand. Yes, sir, I see you.

Fifty thousand. Yes. Sixty. Seventy. Eighty. Eighty thousand for the female of your dreams. Yes, we have eighty thousand. Let's go for the biggie. A hundred thousand. Do we hear a hundred thousand?

(With a flourish, SHEILA opens the clutch bag and firmly holds up the credit card)

PIGG: A hundred thousand pounds. Yes, *madam!*

CRUTNEY: *(Noticing immediately)*: Sheila, put that down!

PIGG: Any advance on a hundred thousand?

CRUTNEY: Sheila? Stop the auction – she's malfunctioning!

PIGG: Going . . .!

CRUTNEY: I said stop the auction! Mr Pigg!

PIGG: Going . . . !

CRUTNEY: Listen you halfwit pommie – she's about to make us both bankrupt!

PIGG: *(Turning slightly towards SHEILA): Gone!*

(PIGG and CRUTNEY freeze. SHEILA calmly replaces the card, places a hand against PIGG's head, and, in slow motion, hurls it with a strong, thrusting motion as though she were

putting a shot. In slow motion, PIGG reels back, tumbles, rolls across the floor, and finally lies still. SHEILA does the same to CRUTNEY, and is just about to make her exit when she turns to pluck a flower from the vase. Passing it under her nose, she smiles, throws it into the audience, then leaves)

A History of Pookie

Characters: 2 principals, at least 3 others
Performance time: 4 minutes

Although much of the humour in A HISTORY OF POOKIE lies in the tension between the storytellers, it is the WORMS with their stocking masks who are most likely to attract attention. The mime outlined below is written for up to four WORMS and may have to be reworked if there are more. That isn't difficult. What matters is to keep the hoots concise, and the poses coordinated, vigorous and imaginative. The sketch, designed as street theatre, uses the metaphor of the arms race to expose the flaws in human communication.

(The WORMS begin the sketch huddled in a group to stage right. They have stockings over their heads, but these are more or less hidden from the audience. They also carry party hooters. THE COMPERE and his ASSISTANT stand forward to stage left, THE COMPERE holding two clipboards, the ASSISTANT two balloons, one of them inflated and tied to the top of his head. He inflates the other while THE COMPERE is making his opening speech)

THE COMPERE: *(Ostentatiously)*: Ladies and gentlemen! For your delight and delectation! It is now our pleasure! To introduce you! A quaint aerobic dumb show! Entitled! An Instant History Of – The Universe!

ASSISTANT: *(Bursting the baloon and spreading his arms wide)*: Boom!

THE COMPERE: *(Almost dead with shock, to the ASSISTANT)*: What was that?

ASSISTANT: Well if this is a history of the universe, then it starts with the Big Bang.

(The ASSISTANT solicits a groan from the audience. THE COMPERE is not amused)

THE COMPERE: For goodness' sake! This is serious theatre.

ASSISTANT: *(Sounding put out)*: Oh, sor-*ry!*

THE COMPERE: Can't you see how engrossed these people are?

ASSISTANT: Okay. I said I'm sorry. *(Patting THE COMPERE's shoulder)*: You carry on.

(With difficulty THE COMPERE returns his attention to the audience. Aside, the ASSISTANT rolls his eyes)

THE COMPERE: From whence, it is asked, did intelligent life originate?

ASSISTANT: *(Shooting his hand up and approaching THE COMPERE)*: Ooh! I know!

THE COMPERE: The question's rhetorical, idiot! I don't need anyone to tell me.

ASSISTANT: But I know the answer!

THE COMPERE: *(Firmly)*: Go away.

(The ASSISTANT retreats, pulling a face)

(Calmly, to the audience): The answer? A galactic back alley, and a little known planet called: Pookie.

ASSISTANT: Pookie?!

THE COMPERE: *(Finally losing control)*: Pookie! Pookie! What's wrong with that? Pookie!

ASSISTANT: It's a stupid name for a planet. That's what's wrong with it.

THE COMPERE: *(Now nose to nose)*: It's colloquial.

ASSISTANT: It sounds like a hamster.

THE COMPERE: *(In restrained exasperation)*: Look. Will you please stop interrupting and read your part. Please.

(THE COMPERE hands his ASSISTANT a clipboard)

ASSISTANT: *(Under compulsion, searching the script)*: Here?

THE COMPERE: Yes. 'In the swamps . . . '

ASSISTANT: *(Reading to the audience)*: In the swamps of 'Pookie' lay deep primeval slime.

(The WORMS slowly rise and unfold, assuming ghastly shapes)

THE COMPERE: And living in the slime, primeval worms.

ASSISTANT: The worms revolved.

(The WORMS, their poses fixed, begin to turn slowly to the right)

THE COMPERE: *E*-volved! *E*-volved!

ASSISTANT: Until they had primitive prehensile tongues.

(The WORMS, who have now turned full circle, simultaneously stick party hooters in their mouths and stand up straight, each with his fingers laced across his chest. This position, like the ones that follow, is held until the next hoot)

THE COMPERE: Half a billion years later they learned how to use them, and called themselves:

WORMS: *HOOT!*

(On the hoot the WORMS stick their thumbs under their lapels, or point to themselves)

ASSISTANT: Which means, worms.

THE COMPERE: They had other words, too. Like:

WORMS: *HOOT!*

(On the hoot the WORMS turn to each other and assume a handshake pose)

ASSISTANT: Meaning peace, and

WORMS: *HOOT!*

(On the hoot the WORMS assume poses of affection, perhaps kissing with their hooters)

THE COMPERE: Meaning love, and

WORMS: *HOOT!*

(On the hoot the WORMS face forward, arms round each other's shoulders, the ones at the ends of the line raising their free hands in a wave)

ASSISTANT: Meaning justice.

THE COMPERE: They said these loudly . . .

WORMS: *(Static): HOOT!*

THE COMPERE: . . . while they made war on each other.

(The WORMS suddenly turn in on someone in the middle of the line and grasp him by the throat. Over the next four hoots they develop and intensify the scene. The impression should be of four still photos taken in quick

succession in the course of a mugging. On the final hoot the victimized WORM is flat on the floor)

ASSISTANT: The rest is history.

THE COMPERE: Julius Caesar!

WORMS: *HOOT!*

ASSISTANT: Fu Manchu!

WORMS: *HOOT!*

THE COMPERE: Ghengis Khan!

WORMS: *HOOT!*

ASSISTANT: Margaret Thatcher! *(Or another appropriate target)*

WORMS: *HOOOOOOOOOT!*

ASSISTANT: That was political.

(The WORMS separate, and stand again, facing forward)

THE COMPERE: *(Having cast the ASSISTANT a warning glance)*: Finally they invented the thermonuclear wormbomb.

ASSISTANT: But who would be first to use it?

THE COMPERE: Of course everyone said:

WORMS: *(Laying their rights hands on their hearts): HOOT!*

ASSISTANT: Meaning, not me!

THE COMPERE: And then –

BOTH: *The climax!*

THE COMPERE: An international incident. At 0800 hours an unidentified object travelling at supersonic speed is picked up on the wormscreens.

(The WORMS put their hands to their brows. They move around, scanning the skies)

ASSISTANT: The defenders open the Hot Wormline to warn massive retaliation.

THE COMPERE: Are your intentions hostile? I repeat. *Are your intentions hostile?*

WORMS: *(Bringing their gazes to rest on THE COMPERE and momentarily freezing): HOOT!*

(Now moving in slow motion, the WORMS take their hands down and begin to creep up menacingly behind THE COMPERE and the ASSISTANT)

THE COMPERE: Pardon?

WORMS: *HOOT!*

ASSISTANT: In the command room sweat trickles down foreheads.

THE COMPERE: Was that yes or no?

ASSISTANT: Can't make it out, sir.

THE COMPERE: Well, fetch the dictionary, you fool. Call yourself a worm?

ASSISTANT: There's only one word *in* the dictionary, sir. One word – eight hundred thousand meanings.

THE COMPERE: Confound it! How are we supposed to communicate when we've only got one word?

ASSISTANT: Ten seconds left, sir.

THE COMPERE: Is it a pre-emptive strike?

ASSISTANT: Five . . .

THE COMPERE: Maybe it's a peace mission!

ASSISTANT: Four . . .

THE COMPERE: An electrical fault on the wormscreen. A UFO.

ASSISTANT: Three . . .

THE COMPERE: Why did I have to be on duty today?

ASSISTANT: Two . . .

THE COMPERE: Darn it, the whole civilization of Pookie could be going down the chute!

ASSISTANT: One . . .

THE COMPERE: Will somebody please tell me if I should press this button?

(By now the WORMS are looming over them like so many Draculas. When the ASSISTANT bursts the second balloon they 'explode' backwards, fall to the ground; but then come forward again, pulling off their stocking masks. As before, THE COMPERE has nearly had a cardiac arrest)

ASSISTANT: Boom!

THE COMPERE: What was that?

ASSISTANT: *(Casually, dusting his palms)*: Like I said before, it's the Big Bang. Say –

EVERYONE: *(The WORMS now standing with THE COMPERE and the ASSISTANT)*: Any more intelligent life around here?

No Strings

Characters: 4
Performance time: 2 minutes

Few sermons in the festive season are allowed to end without a reminder that Christmas means giving. But when the chips are down, how many of us would leave old Santa his mince pie and sherry if he didn't bring a bag of goodies down the chimney?

(ONE, TWO, THREE and FOUR stand in a line, facing front)

ONE: Christmas,

TWO: Pudding,

THREE: Crackers,

FOUR: Turkey,

ONE: Trees,

TWO: Lights,

THREE: Tinsel,

FOUR: Holly,

ALL: *And . . .*

ONE: *(Breaking formation)*: Presents!

TWO: Presence of mind?

ONE: No, presents like this.

(He produces a large Christmas gift, attached to his hand by a string)

TWO: Ooh, how exciting! Thank you so much.

(THREE takes the gift, which ONE immediately pulls back)

ONE: Not so fast. This is a present with strings!

FOUR: What sort of strings?

ONE: Oh, strings like – you could tell me how devastatingly handsome/pretty I look . . .

TWO, THREE, FOUR: *(Lead audience in a groan)*

ONE: Or take me to dinner at the Ritz . . .

TWO, THREE, FOUR: *(Lead audience in a groan)*

ONE: Or give me a bigger present in return . . .

TWO, THREE, FOUR: *(Lead audience in a groan)*

ONE: *(Turning away)*: Suit yourself. No givvy, no takey.

(TWO, THREE and FOUR close ranks, looking at the audience but standing side on)

TWO: Is yours a givvy-takey Christmas?

THREE: Has the stuffing left your stocking?

FOUR: Will 1989 be a cruel Yule?

TWO: If so –

TWO, THREE, FOUR: Give *yourself!*

THREE, FOUR: *(Singing)*:

I'm dreaming of a white Christmas,
Just like the ones I used to know;
Where the treetops glisten, and children listen
To hear sleighbells in the snow (in the snow) . . .

TWO: *(Voice-over the song)*: Be gentle. Be generous. Be kind. Be tolerant of other people's faults, and admiring of their virtues. Always put others first. In short, be the sort of present you yourself would like to receive.

ONE: *(Breaking in)*: That's stupid. I mean it's really wet.

TWO: What's wrong with it?

ONE: Nobody gives himself.

THREE: What do you think Christmas is about?

ONE: *(Taking the audience into the challenge)*: Look. You show me one person in the world who has given himself for others with no strings attached . . .

(TWO, THREE and FOUR look at ONE levelly. He thinks twice)

Okay, okay. There's God. But now show me somebody else . . . !

Three Wise Persons

Characters: 3
Performance Time: 5 minutes

Recent research into ancient Mesopotamian wisdom has unearthed some surprising facts about the Three Wise Men. For a start, MELCHIOR was a woman. (This stands to reason: though of course there was no such thing as camel-lag, men were – as they still are – incapable of arriving anywhere after a long journey and looking presentable.) Secondly, the glib explanation wheeled on in Matthew's gospel – 'We saw his star in the east and have come to worship him' – conceals a complex process of decision-making. In fact the Magi very nearly stayed in Baghdad and put their feet up in front of the telly. What kind of Wise Man is it, after all, who overturns science and reason to accommodate rumours of errant stars and virgins giving birth?

(All three characters wear Christmas cracker hats. On stage, three chairs are placed in a row, facing the audience. MELCHIOR is sitting on the one furthest stage right, filing her nails and reading a magazine. Enter JASPAR)

JASPAR: *(Capering and singing deleriously)*: Oh, you'll never walk . . . a-a-lone, oh you'll never walk . . . Bal-tha-zar, oi-oi-oi, Bal-tha-zar, oi-oi-oi . . . We are the champions, ooh ooh ooh *ooh* ooh . . . !

MELCHIOR: *(Without looking up)*: Did he win?

JASPAR: Did he *win*? He wiped up. 'Balthazar Wiseperson, at the end of that round you have scored ninety-nine points with no passes.' You should have seen the look on Magnus Magnussen's face.

(BALTHAZAR appears stage left, and pauses. He is clearly fed up)

Here's the man. *(Striding over to embrace BALTHAZAR)*: Balthazar of Bhagdad, Mastermind of the Middle East! How does it feel to be the most intelligent man in the world?

BALTHAZAR: *(After a short pause)*: Terrible.

(He breaks free and comes forward to sit next to MELCHIOR)

JASPAR: Come on! You don't mean that.

BALTHAZAR: Oh yes I do.

JASPAR: *(Now standing immediately behind BALTHAZAR)*: But you've been working for this your whole life. What's wrong?

BALTHAZAR: What's wrong, Jaspar, is that I'm bored out of my mind.

JASPAR: Bored . . . ? Melchior, tell him he doesn't mean it.

MELCHIOR: Leave me out of this

BALTHAZAR: You don't realize how depressing life is when you know everything. Nothing's any fun.

JASPAR: What about your telescope? The one I bought you for your five hundredth birthday. You like that.

BALTHAZAR: I used to like it until I realized I could draw a map of the cosmos from memory.

JASPAR: There's Christmas.

BALTHAZAR: Santa Claus doesn't exist.

JASPAR: Bingo?

BALTHAZAR: Jaspar, I cross the numbers off before they've even been called.

JASPAR: Well you never used to win, anyway.

BALTHAZAR: No. But now I *know* I'm not going to win. Come and sit down.

(JASPAR sits down wearily. BALTHAZAR leans forward and proceeds to explain his point)

You see, the problem is: I've discovered the laws.

JASPAR: The laws?

BALTHAZAR: The laws behind the universe.

JASPAR: So?

BALTHAZAR: So I know exactly what's going to happen, years in advance. I mean, its very useful for things like the Stockmarket, don't get me wrong. But it makes day to day living so dull. Do you know how long it's been since I had a real *bona fide* surprise? For example. In exactly two seconds Melchior will remember she's left the bread in the oven.

MELCHIOR: *(Dropping the magazine and sitting up)*: Crikey – the bread!

BALTHAZAR: The she'll notice there's no smell of burning.

MELCHIOR: Oh – thank goodness.

BALTHAZAR: And finally she'll remember who it was who promised he'd fix the timer . . .

MELCHIOR: *(Turning towards JASPAR, hotly)*: Jaspar, you dummy! What are we supposed to eat for lunch!

(In order, the three now assume the following static positions. Remembering his promise, JASPAR immediately claps his hands to his mouth. BALTHAZAR flicks his eyes skyward, and with a sighing motion lays his hands on his cheeks, palms inward. MELCHIOR gives a groan and spreads her hands over her face. They hold the 'three wise monkey' pose for two seconds, then break simultaneously, BALTHAZARgiving the cue by sighing and letting his hands slide down to his

lap. The others follow suit. BALTHAZAR looks resigned; MELCHIOR cross; JASPAR sheepish)

BALTHAZAR: *(Shrugging)*: There's no hope for me. I'd take an overdose if I didn't know I was going to live another thousand years.

(At this JASPAR suddenly frowns, as though taken by inspiration. MELCHIOR stands, putting the magazine down on her chair)

MELCHIOR: Well, it's going to be locust sandwich without the sandwich. Everybody happy?

JASPAR: Wait! Wait – I've got an idea. Balthazar's right. We need a challenge.

MELCHIOR: Dung beetle sandwich?

JASPAR: No, no, no. Business! Commercial success! Imagine it . . . *(Jumping eagerly to his feet, he mimes a sign stage left)*: A massive illuminated sign. Rent – A – Brain – P – L – C. Infallible forecasts. Devastating detail. Reasonable rates. And television ads featuring the world's most intelligent man . . .

(He clicks his fingers and begins an improvised dance routine, singing to the tune Teddybears' Picnic, with

*double handclaps – ** – after the second and fourth lines. MELCHIOR and BALTHAZAR watch him)*

If you go down to the East today
*You're in for a big surprise. ***
You'll meet three people the critics agree
*are unbelievably wise. ***
Jaspar, Melchi and Balthazar
Exceed mere home computers by far:
Today's the day the Wise Men go into biiiz-niss!
(Yeah!)

If you go down to the East today
*You'll never be quite the same. ***
*Compared to our lightning service British Telecom looks quite tame. ***
So if you want your future divined,
Your fortune told, then bear it in mind:
Today's the day the Wise Men go into biiiz-niss!
(Hey!)

(He finishes in an 'Ole' position, arms outstretched, then turns his head to the others)

What do you think?

(A short pause. MELCHIOR and BALTHAZAR look at one another)

MELCHIOR: *(Turning)*: I'm off to butter the locusts.

JASPAR: You didn't like it?

MELCHIOR: Jaspar, it's sexist drivel. Wise *men*!

(She leaves. JASPAR watches her go, and sits down heavily)

BALTHAZAR: Face it, Jaspar. Intelligence is tedium.

JASPAR: Maybe you're right. *(He sighs)*: Pass us that magazine, will you?

BALTHAZAR: *(Passing it, and glancing at the cover)*: The Old Bore's Almanac, 0 BC. I can tell you what it says. December 15th, 7.30 pm – Eastenders.

JASPAR: *(Now consulting the magazine)*: Nope. You're wrong. 'New star appears in sky, heading westward'.

BALTHAZAR: It doesn't say that!

JASPAR: 'Countdown begins to birth of Jewish Messiah – Son of God, Creator of the World, etc., etc. See Old Testament.'

BALTHAZAR: *(Snatching the magazine, to check)*: Give it here.

JASPAR: It's word for word.

BALTHAZAR: Well, well, well. In half a millenium I've never known the Old Bore get it wrong.

JASPAR: Maybe it's you who've got it wrong.

BALTHAZAR: Jaspar, there is no such thing as a new star. New stars don't just turn up out of the blue. It's not scientific. In fact I'd go so far as to say that if there's a new star in the sky this evening, I'll eat my hat.

(MELCHIOR rushes back on stage)

MELCHIOR: Aaaaaaaaaggghhhh!

(She stops by the chair she was sitting on. JASPAR and BALTHAZAR run to support her, one at each elbow)

(Almost beside herself): It's here!

BALTHAZAR: What's here?

MELCHIOR: Coming towards us!

JASPAR: Coming towards us?

(JASPAR and BALTHAZAR stare into the distance, where MELCHIOR is pointing)

MELCHIOR: It's as big as the moon!

JASPAR: As bright as the lights in Blackpool!

BALTHAZAR: Flying three times the speed of sound!

MELCHIOR: Duck!

(They duck, then turn to watch the 'star' fly away backstage. All three face forward again, and there is a short pause)

BALTHAZAR: It's just an aeroplane.

MELCHIOR: It's a star, and you know it. Where's my Old Bore?

(She wrestles the magazine away from BALTHAZAR,

who is now frowning and drumming his fingers on his lips)

JASPAR: What do we do?

MELCHIOR: We follow it. That's what you're supposed to do with stars.

JASPAR: How do you know?

MELCHIOR: Look, sonny. I've been following Barry Manilow for years. He's a star. Wise *men* – Hmph! *(Shoving the magazine into JASPAR's hands)*: Right. You go to the store room and fetch some gold, some frankincense, and some myrrh. Got that? I'll take the camels out of the garage.

(She begins to leave, stage right. JASPAR calls after her)

JASPAR: Where are we going?

MELCHIOR: *(Just before she disappears)*: Just trust me. Female intuition. Okay?

JASPAR: Okay . . .

(JASPAR pauses, puts an arm round BALTHAZAR)

JASPAR: So, Mr Know-it-all. What have you got to say for yourself?

BALTHAZAR: Okay, so I made one small mistake.

JASPAR: A surprise, eh?

(JASPAR releases him, snatches the hat off

BALTHAZAR's head and offers it to him. As JASPAR leaves, BALTHAZAR slowly lifts the hat, and looks at it)

BALTHAZAR: Yes. Well, what would life be without surprises?

(He smiles, stuffs the hat into his mouth, and leaves)

A Special Case

Characters: 5
Performance time: 5 minutes

Everyman is a character with a long and distinguished history on the English stage. Here we catch him in one of his down moments, as GEORGE Thingummy, husband to ANGELA and father of TADPOLE, who though affecting grandeur is a self-evident nondescript with about as much mettle as a bowl of custard. But GEORGE isn't the central character; that place belongs to THE DEVIL, a pantomime villain who alternately threatens and confides in the audience, and whose villainy is therefore as appealing as his downfall. The family group has its own internal dynamic, ANGELA being the dominant character, and TADPOLE a slightly awkward appendage. Though TADPOLE is an infant, the family's absurdity will be heightened if he is played by an adult.

(Enter THE DEVIL, complete with horns. He stumbles on the audience slightly stage left)

THE DEVIL: Ah! Humans! What a *nice* surprise! And I can see by those cheeky, cheerful smiles, you're just racing down that broad road which leadeth to destruction! Aren't you, you naughty people? *(Approaching a victim)*: Here's one at the head of the pack. Tasteless colour of tie you've got there, sir. Won't be sorry to see that burned up, will we? That and the toupé. And are you still on the run from the Inland Revenue? What a rogue! And overdoing the booze and the red meat? Good. Won't be long before we see you again. An example to shame the worst of us!

GEORGE: *(Breaking in)*: Hello!

(Enter GEORGE, from stage right, ANGELA and TADPOLE close behind him. All three are in garish beachwear – TADPOLE perhaps with a nappy and bathcap)

THE DEVIL: *(After glancing at GEORGE, to the audience)*: Aha! Excuse me.

GEORGE: *(Coming forward)*: Fancy dress party going on here?

THE DEVIL: *(To the audience)*: My favourite kind of person – an idiot. *(Turning to GEORGE)*: No. Can I help you?

(GEORGE thrusts out a hand which THE DEVIL shakes without enthusiasm. ANGELA and TADPOLE follow in after GEORGE)

GEORGE: George Thingummy. I'm looking for a place called The Other Side.

THE DEVIL: Rest assured, Mr Thingummy, you are almost there. *(Catching sight of ANGELA and TADPOLE)*: Oh – but there are more of you!

GEORGE: Yes. My wife, Angela.

ANGELA: *(Coming forward, with TADPOLE in tow)*: How d'y do.

THE DEVIL: And what a *charming* child . . .

GEORGE: That's Tadpole.

THE DEVIL: *(Stooping, playfully squeezing TADPOLE's cheek)*: Oh, you're snack size, aren't you? Yes, you are!

(TADPOLE blows a raspberry, to which THE DEVIL replies in kind. This is not seen by GEORGE and ANGELA, and he straightens with a winsome smile)

(To GEORGE and ANGELA): Now I trust you've made a booking?

GEORGE: They're expecting us at the Hotel Excelsior de la Eternal Bliss.

THE DEVIL: But what a coincidence! *(With a confiding glance at the audience)*: I am the proprietor of that selfsame institution. *(He guides them forward)*: If you would just like to join the rest of the party, we are on our way there.

ANGELA: *(Catching sight of the audience)*: Oh George, I don't like the look of *them*.

THE DEVIL: Is something the matter?

GEORGE: I think this must be a different tour. These people here are . . . *ordinary*.

THE DEVIL: Ah, silly me! And I should have

known by looking at you that you are – special. Is that right?

GEORGE: That's right.

THE DEVIL: That's *right*. Well the situation is not beyond repair.

*(He beckons them close.
TADPOLE tips his head
back to look up at them)*

Granted that you, George and Angela, have evolved on to a higher plane of being – nonetheless you, and they, have a common ancestor.

GEORGE: Are you telling me I'm descended from a dinosaur?

THE DEVIL: If I remember rightly, his name was Adam. He was your great great great great great great great great great great great grandfather.

ANGELA: George! He's the one who left us that fig leaf bottled in ether!

GEORGE: *(To THE DEVIL)*: You're joking! This bunch is descended from Great Grandpa Adam?

THE DEVIL: Like frogs from fish.

ANGELA: *(Gluttonously, at the audience)*: Relatives!

GEORGE: Angela, for goodness sake! Don't you realize what this means? If they're our relatives, we're not special any more are we?

ANGELA: *(Transfixed)*: Who cares? Where there's relatives, there's babies!

(She rubs her hands together in anticipation. THE DEVIL steps in)

THE DEVIL: The practical wisdom of a woman. Now come along, everyone, otherwise we shall all be late for dinner.

GEORGE: I'm not moving.

ANGELA: George! *(To THE DEVIL)*: He can be very stubborn.

GEORGE: If I can't be special, I'm staying right here.

THE DEVIL: Oh now George – don't be so hasty. *(Taking him aside)*: How about you and me doing a little deal? You come down to the hotel, and I'll turn you into something so special you'll make Arnold Schwarzneggar look like a traffic warden.

ANGELA: Do it, George.

GEORGE: How much will it cost?

THE DEVIL: *(Placing a pen and contract in GEORGE's hand)*: Virtually nothing. You sign this paper giving me exclusive rights to your soul, and I make you a special person for the rest of your life. Can't say fairer than that.

ANGELA: Hurry up and sign it, you twit. We can't hang around here forever.

(GEORGE signs the contract. THE DEVIL pockets it and then studies his watch)

THE DEVIL: Good. Now we'll just wait a moment or two . . .

ANGELA: Can't we go right away?

THE DEVIL: Not until he has his heart attack.

GEORGE, ANGELA: Heart attack!

GEORGE: *(To THE DEVIL)*: Now wait a minute. That wasn't in the contract.

THE DEVIL: George, you told me not two minutes ago that you wanted to go to the Other Side.

GEORGE: But not on my own!

THE DEVIL: *(Getting out the form again with an air of weary compliance)*: Okay, we'll have three heart attacks. It's all the same to me.

ANGELA: We don't want *any* heart attacks.

THE DEVIL: You don't . . . *(Feigning consternation)*: Ah, silly me! You were looking for the *other* Hotel Excelsior!

GEORGE, ANGELA: The *other* Hotel Excelsior!

THE DEVIL: I forget the name of the owner. Almighty somebody.

ANGELA: God.

THE DEVIL: Almighty God. Of course. No, you wouldn't have liked it there. Too common for you.

ANGELA: But we made a booking.

THE DEVIL: With me. Exactly.

GEORGE: No.

THE DEVIL: Well what's the difference?

ANGELA: We want our money's worth!

THE DEVIL: *(Losing patience)*: Oh humans! Winge, winge, winge. Throw them into boiling lava, and what do you get? Winge, winge, winge! Well it's no good moaning. You signed the contract, and like it or not you're on your way to the Big Sauna.

(THE DEVIL again studies his watch. GEORGE, ANGELA AND TADPOLE look panicky)

GEORGE: Help!

THE DEVIL: Three . . .

ANGELA: God!

THE DEVIL: Two . . .

GEORGE: Do something!

THE DEVIL: *(His finger poised)*: One . . .

OFFICIAL: *(Off stage)*: Hello-o!

THE DEVIL: Oh blast!

(GEORGE, ANGELA and TADPOLE turn in the direction of the voice. The OFFICIAL marches on from stage right, a clipboard in his hand)

OFFICIAL: George Angela and Tadpole Thingummy?

GEORGE, ANGELA: Yes?

OFFICIAL: *(Shaking hands)*: Celestial Tours.

THE DEVIL: *(Scornfully, aside to the audience)*: 'Celestial Tours. Dial seven three seven for your passage to heaven.' Huh! *(He gets out his contract)*

OFFICIAL: You made a booking with us for the Excelsior?

ANGELA: That's right.

THE DEVIL: *(Breaking in)*: Not so fast. These people agreed to come with me.

(He shoves the contract into the OFFICIAL's hand. The OFFICIAL peruses it)

OFFICIAL: Well, George and Angela, this all seems to turn on your status . . .

THE DEVIL: Precisely. And they're *special – aren't* you, George and Angela?

OFFICIAL: What do you say, George?

GEORGE: *(Clearly flattered)*: Well I suppose it can't be denied that we're not quite –

ANGELA: *(Sharply)*: George!

GEORGE: *(Suddenly limp)*: – that we're just regular, run-of-the-mill, ordinary human beings.

OFFICIAL: That'll do nicely.

(ANGELA punches GEORGE on the arm for having almost got it wrong)

If you'd like to get on the bus . . .

(The OFFICIAL indicates the bus, off stage right, and

ANGELA leads GEORGE away. He then tears the contract in half, dropping the pieces at THE DEVIL's feet, and ushers TADPOLE off)

THE DEVIL: *(Calling after them petulantly)*: Prove it! Go on! Where's your documentation? I'll have you for breach of contract!

(TADPOLE, remaining at the edge of the stage, turns to face him and blows another raspberry)

(Making to give chase): Rrrrrr!

(TADPOLE retreats off stage right, and THE DEVIL stops, glaring after him. He composes himself and turns to the audience, his expression severe)

I'll see you – later!

(He strides off)

The Scoop

Characters: 2
Performance time: 3 minutes

In the Gospel according to Matthew the priests and the Pharisees have a hard time keeping the lid on the Resurrection story. How did they manage it? This suggestion may not be historically accurate, but it does reflect the interests of the various groups concerned. It can simply be read, or acted with, say, TALMUD sitting at his writing desk and SENECA reclining in a raffia chair with an iced bacardi in his hand.

SENECA: To the Temple Executive; Dear sir. As Middle East correspondent for the *Rome Tribune* I am required to report on events surrounding Jesus of Nazareth, executed in Jerusalem last Friday, and to this end it would be of great assistance to me, not to say a service to the Empire of Rome, if I could be granted a short audience with the Chief Priest. I look forward to hearing from you. Yours sincerely, Lucius Seneca.

TALMUD: Dear Mr Seneca. I regret to inform you that the Chief Priest is at present on holiday in Gaza. If I can help you in any way I shall be most glad to do so, provided, of course, that you undertake not to publish anything detrimental to the interests of the state. As to Jesus of Nazareth, it is well known hereabouts that nothing worthy of note ever emanated from that part of the country. Yours respectfully, Joshua Talmud, Head Scribe.

SENECA: Dear Mr Talmud. I am grateful for your offer of assistance. Other sources have suggested to me that this Jesus was a worker of miracles, and ultimately became the victim of a political assassination. Are you in a position to comment on this? Yours sincerely.

TALMUD: Dear Mr Seneca. No, I am not in a position to comment. Suffice it to say that Jesus was a self-proclaimed peacenik who spent his spare hours ransacking temple shops. Caesar was right – for once – when he said you could judge a man by the length of his hair. Yours respectfully.

SENECA: Dear Mr Talmud. I take your point. However: if, as you suggest, Jesus of Nazareth was little more than a common criminal, why was it considered necessary to put a praetorian guard on his tomb? Yours sincerely.

TALMUD: Dear Mr Seneca. If your sources were as informed as you seem to think they are, they would have told you of the claims made by this Jesus – among his numerous Messaianic ravings – that he would rise from the dead. It doesn't take even the average Roman's intelligence to see that some of the

	man's followers might be tempted to 'assist' his resurrection, or that measures must be taken to ensure the dead stay dead. Yours respectfully.
SENECA:	Dear Mr Talmud. You are too generous to the Roman intellect. Nonetheless, as I am sure you are aware, the tomb donated for the man's burial by Joseph of Arimithea is now empty. I take it there is an official explanation for this? Yours sincerely.
TALMUD:	Dear Mr Seneca, there is indeed an official explanation. The body was stolen by the man's followers last Saturday evening and buried elsewhere. Which is why we are now being treated to the embarrassing spectacle of tax-collectors and prostitutes preaching at every street corner as though they were the darlings of the true Messiah. I need hardly stress to you the political dangers of such a claim. Yours respectfully.
SENECA:	Dear Mr Talmud. I have talked to some of the followers of whom you wrote. They do not strike me as particularly clever or well-connected, and to my mind this casts some doubt on your assertion that they overwhelmed a trained Roman guard in order to dispose of the corpse.
TALMUD:	Dear Mr Seneca. To my mind nothing is more unremarkable.
SENECA:	Dear Mr Talmud. Very funny. In that case perhaps you would like to tell me

why you personally were seen on the Monday after the resurrection paying the same guards three months' wages for a single night's work. Considering that they failed in the one duty you employed them to perform, this is either an unprecedented gesture of goodwill towards the occupying forces, or a bungled attempt at a cover-up. I have no doubt that readers of the *Tribune* will incline to the latter view.

TALMUD: Dear . . . Lucius. Let us tread carefully. I do not pretend to be a paragon of virtue; in return, however, may I remind you that the last Middle East correspondent to rake about in the muck of provincial affairs was withdrawn at the express wish of the Emperor, and now works as a goat handler in an obscure part of Gaul?

SENECA: Dear . . . Joshua. I think I catch the drift of your thought. May I suggest that we meet for dinner some time this week and come to an agreement that will achieve for this resurrection story the oblivion it deserves?

TALMUD: Dear Lucius. You show the pragmatism for which Romans are admired the world over. I commend you. In fact with the Feast of Pentecost coming up I dare say that so far as the news media are concerned the resurrection will die a natural death. Still, it calls for a small celebration. Shall we say Levi's Muttonburger Joint, Thursday at six?

Ballad of the Cake Diggers

Characters: 1 principal, at least 4 others
Performance time: 2 minutes

Like BOATING FOR GOPHERS, the BALLAD OF THE CAKE DIGGERS is a form of rap. But since in this case there is only one principal part, the rhythm, which is an unbroken 4/4 time from start to finish, must be kept by the BALLADEER. Further explanations, and suggestions for a rough choreography, are footnoted so as not to interfere with the layout of the text. As a sort of children's parable on world economics, the BALLAD focuses on the need to conserve non-renewable resources and demonstrates that in environmental terms you can't, so to speak, have your cake and eat it. With apologies to Marie Antoinette . . .

(The GIVERS and the TAKERS stand in close formation, in two groups. Between them is the BALLADEER, who coordinates and conducts)

ALL: *We're from the country*
of Give and Take,
And we all hate potatoes
and we all eat cake! Eat cake! Eat cake![1]

BALLADEER: Now – here we have the Givers (as you see, they're very thin),

GIVERS: *THIN!*[2]

BALLADEER: Weedy arms, weedy legs,
and spots across their chins.

GIVERS: *CHINS!*[3]

BALLADEER: The fat ones on the other side
are Takers – am I right?

TAKERS: *YES!*[4]

BALLADEER: You'll always tell the Takers
'cause their trousers are too tight!

TAKERS: *OW!*

BALLADEER: They're not exactly light, either!

ALL: *We're from the country*
of Give and Take,
And we all hate potatoes
and we all eat cake! Eat cake! Eat cake!

BALLADEER: Now this cake is very strange. You see, it's mined underground.

GIVERS: DIG *DIG* DIG *DIG!*[5]

BALLADEER: Then it's taken to the Takers who consume it by the pound.

TAKERS: PIG *PIG* PIG *PIG!*[6]

BALLADEER: When the Takers are fed, they're nearly fifty times as fat.

GIVERS, TAKERS: BIG *BIG* BIG *BIG*[7]

BALLADEER: But the Givers – all the Givers get is crumbs! Think of that!

GIVERS, TAKERS: *WOW!*

ALL: *We're from the country*
of Give and Take,
And we all hate potatoes
and we all eat cake! Eat cake! Eat cake!

BALLADEER: Now – twenty thousand crumbs
hardly make a decent meal.

TAKERS: CHOMP *CHOMP* CHOMP *CHOMP!*[8]

BALLADEER: So if you're a Giver digger it's
a pretty crummy deal.

GIVERS: STOMP *STOMP* STOMP *STOMP!*[9]

BALLADEER: But the Takers aren't dumb – they say
do overtime too.
More cake for us,[10]
more crumbs for you! Because:

ALL: *We're from the country*
of Give and Take,
And we all hate potatoes
and we all eat cake! Eat cake! Eat cake!

BALLADEER: So the Givers go a-slaving[11]
and the Takers stand about,
And they both eat cake until
the cake runs out.

GIVERS, TAKERS: *WHAT?*[12]

BALLADEER: The cake runs out! You know:
run run *run* run *run* run *run!*[13]
There must be something else you eat
. . . ? Bread?

GIVERS, TAKERS: *NO!*[14]

BALLADEER: Tongue?

GIVERS, TAKERS: *NO!*

BALLADEER: Sticky currant buns?

GIVERS, TAKERS: *NO!*

BALLADEER: Beef?

GIVERS,
TAKERS: *NO!*

BALLADEER: Granola?

GIVERS,
TAKERS: *NO!*

BALLADEER: Diet Coca-Cola?

GIVERS,
TAKERS: *NO!*

BALLADEER: Eggs?

GIVERS,
TAKERS: *NO!*

BALLADEER: Ham?

GIVERS,
TAKERS: *NO!*

BALLADEER: Vinegar and clams?

GIVERS,
TAKERS: *NO!*

BALLADEER: Cheese?

GIVERS,
TAKERS: *NO!*

BALLADEER: Tomatoes?

GIVERS,
TAKERS: *NO!*

BALLADEER: And never baked potatoes!

ALL: *Oh – we're from the country*
of Give and Take,
And we all hate potatoes
and we all eat cake!

Yes, we're from the country
of Give and Take,
And we all hate potatoes
and we all eat cake! Eat cake! Eat . . .

(The GIVERS and the TAKERS simultaneously clutch their stomachs, as if suddenly poisoned, and collapse)

BALLADEER: Cake?

Notes:

1 The same series of actions is performed by everyone during the refrain. 'We're' is accompanied by the index finger of the right hand pointing at the chest. On 'Give' the same hand is fully extended, open with palm upward, and on 'Take' immediately withdrawn, clenched, to the chest. Both hands are raised to shoulder height on the first 'all', with fingers spread and palms facing out, and then swung down and patted against the stomach for the second 'all' and every repetition of 'cake'.
2 The GIVERS close their palms together to illustrate thinness.
3 Thrusting out their chins and pointing at them with both index fingers.
4 Spoken with an emphatic nod, after which the TAKERS pull their shoulders back and look conceited. The pose is broken, with an expression of pain, on the *OW!*
5 Metrically this line begins with the second DIG and not the first, hence the italicisation. The GIVERS are bending forward, swinging shovels into an imaginary pile of sand. The shovel goes in twice, on the second and fourth DIGs.
6 Metrical pattern as above. The actions here are sloppy scooping motions that bring cupped palms up to the mouth, left and right, left and right.
7 Metrical pattern as above. Adopting a 'fat' posture, GIVERS and TAKERS spread their hands over their stomachs. With each BIG they move the hands further out, as though being inflated like a balloon.
8 Metrical pattern as above. It is the TAKERS who do the eating. This time they hold both arms out straight, imitating crocodile jaws. The jaws open and close, open and close.

9 Metrical pattern as above. Close-fisted, the GIVERS swing their arms as though marching, left right, left right.

10 This is accompanied by symbolic gestures from the TAKERS. On 'us' they point at themselves, on 'you' they point at the GIVERS.

11 Over the next four lines the GIVERS swing their shovels to the on-beat.

12 In total disbelief, looking at the BALLADEER.

13 The BALLADEER demonstrates.

14 The *NO*s in this section fall consistently on the off-beat. After 'potatoes' the *NO!* is replaced by a 'Oh' leading directly into the refrain.

Shinlick and Trash

Characters: 2
Performance time: 3 minutes

An audience will generally find satire funny as long as they share a common enemy with the performer. Satirizing agnosticism in street theatre therefore has its problems, for the audience themselves, and not some third party like the Government or the church, are ultimately the butt of the humour. SHINLICK and TRASH get around this by directing the satire at themselves and tactfully ignoring any sympathy the audience may have with their point of view. Although written as two parts the piece involves virtually no direct interaction of the speakers, and should be thought of as a monologue.

(SHINLICK and TRASH are dressed like insurance salespersons: smart, formal, dark. Both have large books under their arms)

SHINLICK: We know what *you're* thinking!

TRASH: You're thinking:

BOTH: *Mormons!*

TRASH: Go on – be honest, you were, weren't you?

SHINLICK: And you were getting worried because you thought we were going to wallop you one over the head with our Mormon Bibles and drag you away to a Mormon church where they wire people up to million volt Frankenstein machines and turn them into Mormons. Weren't you?

TRASH: Well you're wrong! We know what it's like to be done over by Mormons and Hare Krishnas and Baltic pig worshippers, and we're striking back. We trail Jehovah's Witnesses to their homes, and we creep up to their doors at midnight and ring the bell and shout:

BOTH: Wanna read a magazine about agnosticism?

SHINLICK: You see, we think it's high time agnosticism went on the offensive. Agnosticism is the religion of the future. Completely flexible. Doesn't tie you to anything specific. And at the same time commends you as broad-minded and tolerant of other people's views. He's a Hindu. She's a Thomist.

TRASH: And the dog's into gestalt therapy. We make no distinctions, the agnostic welcomes all. Just make sure you don't invite Botha and Boesak to the same dinner party. Oh, and nice to see you, General Pinochet. Pink gin? Yes – if you'd just leave the body bag outside . . . ?

SHINLICK: Of course the major selling point of agnosticism is its *intellectual integrity*. None of this namby-pambying around with metaphysics. If anyone comes up with that old existential brainteaser 'Why are you alive?', the answer is: you don't know.

TRASH: In fact for the agnostic that's the answer to most things. You don't know, we don't know, nobody knows, and everybody's happy. To be an agnostic, all you have to do is remember the golden rule:

BOTH: Not knowing is no excuse for trying to find out!

SHINLICK: Because if you found out, you wouldn't be an agnostic any more, would you? Needless to say, avoid the Mormons. And never,

TRASH: ever,

SHINLICK: ever,

TRASH: ever,

SHINLICK: go near a Christian church. They may try and bore you to death but underneath they're subversives. Any religion that pulls together peace, love, Resurrection and social justice under one roof must be off the deep end. And remember, if anyone asks you in, there's always a good reason for refusing:

TRASH: Think what your friends will say!

SHINLICK: What –

TRASH: you?

SHINLICK: Church?

TRASH: Never.

SHINLICK: You're kidding.

TRASH: Really?

BOTH: What – a – wally!

SHINLICK: Works every time. Now – anything you want to ask us before we go?

TRASH: No?

SHINLICK: Yes! *Is Christianity true?* Oh, very astute!

TRASH: A classic question,

SHINLICK: deserving a classic answer. To be honest – we don't know . . .

BOTH: *(They turn to each other)*: do we?

Lonesome Bonesome

Characters: 3 puppets (2 puppeteers), at least 6 others
Performance time: about 25 minutes

Every dog has his day, and LONESOME BONESOME is the story of MUTTSY's day – to be precise, his birthday. The only trouble is, MUTTSY's too depressed to enjoy it. But what's wrong? And what can be done by the famous dogologist DR Woof Woof BARK to set things right?

This salutary tale of teenage angst is a puppet play designed for a cast of up to twenty people. Only two are needed to operate the puppets (MUTTSY, JEANIE, and DR BARK); the others (the NARRATOR, MRS PINKERTON, and the ACTORS) are positioned to the sides of the screen, and for much of the time related to the puppet characters as though in the audience. They are distinguished from the audience in two respects: first that they talk to the puppets, and second that they come on at the beginning as if to present a show. The show – whatever it might have been – never happens, and the rest of the play is really a sort of casual digression.

LONESOME BONESOME is meant to be simple. The minimum requirements are as follows: (1) three hand puppets, two of them (MUTTSY and JEANIE) recognizable as dogs; (2) some sort of puppet stage; (3) an adult guitarist-anchorperson to be the NARRATOR; and (4) a couple of people – probably not less than 14 years old – to be puppeteers (one for MUTTSY, the other for JEANIE, DR BARK and the voice of the HOUND OF HEAVEN). The rest of the characters are referred to collectively in the script as the ACTORS, and cover the other five speaking parts: MRS PINKERTON and the speaking ACTORS (1, 2, 3 and 4), all of whom can be played by older children or young teenagers. It may assist in creating a mood of easy informality if the ACTORS carry puppets or stuffed toys of their own.

No particular music is suggested for the beginning and end of the play. Songs on the theme of teenage love aren't hard to find, and most groups will have their own favourites. Of the two songs included in the script, one, **Dem Bones**, *is traditional. The score to* **I dream of Jeanie**, *by Steven Foster, can be found in the* EMI Book of PARLOUR SONGS, *compiled by Ian Wallace and published in 1981 by EMI Music Publishing Ltd.*

(The screen, with the puppeteers behind it, is placed centrally with a chair adjacent, stage right. A second chair is placed in front and slightly stage left, other furniture at the sides, far enough forward that the ACTORS who will sit there can see the action. The ACTORS are led on by the NARRATOR, who introduces the opening song. This is performed standing up. If the audience has an ounce of common decency they will applaud, and at this point the NARRATOR takes his seat on the chair to stage right, and the ACTORS divide to sit informally on the furniture at the sides: MRS PINKERTON and ACTORS 2 and 4 to stage left, ACTORS 1 and 3 to stage right)

NARRATOR: Thank you, and now we want to introduce you to the star of our show, a dog with the biggest smile on Broadway, a dog who's been the life and soul of every rehearsal. (*To the* ACTORS): Hasn't Muttsy cheered us up these last few days?

ACTORS: Yes!

NARRATOR: And we'll let you in on a secret. This is Muttsy's birthday! Will you help us sing happy birthday to him? *(He encourages the audience to join in, and leads the singing)*:

NARRATOR, ACTORS:
Happy birthday to you,
Happy birthday to you,
Happy birthday, dear Muttsy,
Happy birthday to you!

(Applause as MUTTSY appears. He looks glum)

NARRATOR: Happy birthday, Muttsy.

MUTTSY: *(Sighing dolefully)*: Thanks.

ACTOR 1: Are you all right, Muttsy?

MUTTSY: *(Sighing and shaking his head)*: Oh me oh my.

ACTOR 2: What's wrong with him?

NARRATOR: I don't know. Muttsy, we've just given you the big build-up. We've told all these people what a happy person you are.

MUTTSY: *(To the audience)*: He's lying.

NARRATOR: Muttsy! What's got into you?

ACTOR 1: I think he's been to a disco.

ACTOR 3: Me too. You hate discos, don't you, Muttsy?

MUTTSY: Yeah. Discos give me a headache. They make my ears curl and teeth fall out.

(A puppeteer throws some tooth-shaped pieces of cardboard over the screen)

You should know by now that I'd rather eat Kit-e-kat ice cream than go to a disco.

NARRATOR: So what's the matter?

MUTTSY: *(Sighing)*: You really want to know?

ACTOR 2: Yes, we do.

MUTTSY: Nobody loves me.

NARRATOR, ACTORS: Nobody loves you?

MUTTSY: That's what I said. Nobody loves me.

ACTOR 3: Who's going to show Muttsy we love him?

ACTOR 4: I will!

(ACTOR 4, a girl, goes and sits down on the chair in front of the stage)

Muttsy – I just wanted to say how much I love and admire you.

MUTTSY: *(To NARRATOR)*: See? It's awful. I'm totally ignored.

NARRATOR: But she's talking to you!

MUTTSY: I used to think I was such a lovable dog. I used to think people meant it when they paid me compliments . . .

ACTOR: *(Persisting)*: And I must say that's a fine bowtie you're wearing!

MUTTSY: Thanks. *(To NARRATOR)*: See? She hates me. They all hate me.

ACTOR 4: In fact . . . Muttsy, would you mind if I gave you a special . . . birthday kiss?

MUTTSY: Oh, I suppose not.

(He holds out his cheek. She kisses him, jumps up and returns to her place. MUTTSY is unmoved)

MUTTSY: *(Tipping his head back)*: Why me, Lord?

NARRATOR: Muttsy. I think you should see someone about this. You're not your normal self.

MUTTSY: Who am I going to see? My Fairy Dogmother?

ACTOR 1: Just see a doctor.

ACTOR 3: Go to the health centre and see Dr Bark.

MUTTSY: *(For the first time showing signs of interest)*: Dr Woof Woof Bark, the famous dogologist?

NARRATOR: That's the one. He'll sort you out, no trouble.

MUTTSY: You think so?

NARRATOR: We're certain. Aren't we?

ACTORS: Positive!

NARRATOR: Here, I'll dial the number for you.

(He dials on a telephone – real or imaginary – and holds the receiver to MUTTSY's ear)

MUTTSY: I hope you're right. Hello! Hello? Is that Doctor Bark? . . . Oh, sorry . . . Well, could I make an appointment with him? . . . Yeah, I'm really sick. Critical *(He coughs lavishly)*: . . . No – not *that* sick . . . No, really . . . No, I don't need an ambulance . . . Hello? Hello!

NARRATOR, ACTORS: (*Led by the NARRATOR)*: Neenaw, neenaw, neenaw, etc.

(To the accompaniment of this ambulance noise ACTOR 3 gets up, grabs MUTTSY by the ears and carries him round the room, dropping him behind the screen. The ambulance noise is faded out, and DR BARK appears)

DR BARK: Next!

(Re-enter MUTTSY)

MUTTSY: Are you Dr Bark, the famous dogologist?

DR BARK: None famouser.

MUTTSY: Could I see you for a moment?

DR BARK: Well be quick. I've got to see my next patient. Next!

MUTTSY: I am your next patient!

DR BARK: Oh. So what seems to be the trouble? Hm?

MUTTSY: I'm sick.

DR BARK: Sick as a dog?

NARRATOR, ACTORS: *(Groan)*

MUTTSY: You put your finger on it, Doc.

DR BARK: I knew it. Open up. Say Aah.

MUTTSY: Aaaaaaaah.

DR BARK: Just what I thought.

MUTTSY: What's wrong with me, Doc?

DR BARK: Everything.

(At this news the NARRATOR and ACTORS look surprised and concerned)

Does it hurt?

MUTTSY: No.

DR BARK: That proves it. Your nerves aren't working. If you were all right, you'd know you were sick.

MUTTSY: What should I do, Doc?

DR BARK: If I were you, I'd see a doctor as soon as possible.

MUTTSY: But I already have seen a doctor!

DR BARK: You have? What did he say?

MUTTSY: That I had everything wrong with me and my nerves weren't working.

DR BARK: He was dead right. Always worth taking a second opinion.

MUTTSY: But Doc . . .

DR BARK: Yep?

MUTTSY: I don't think it's just a medical problem, Doc. I'm sick at heart.

NARRATOR, ACTORS: Sick at *heart!*

MUTTSY: Lonesome.

DR BARK: Aha! Then I'll tell you what you need. You need a girlfriend.

NARRATOR, ACTORS: *(Wolf whistles and laughter)*

MUTTSY: Can I get one on the National Health?

DR BARK: Not a very good one. If you take my advice, you'll go private. A computer dating agency. You give the agency your personal details, and they'll find someone who's perfectly suited for you.

MUTTSY: *(Giving an appreciative bark)*: You know, I've never had a girlfriend.

DR BARK: Never too late to start.

MUTTSY: Can you recommend an agency?

DR BARK: Come with me, an' I'll put you in touch with the very best. The Dog Day Dating Service. It's run by a lady called Mrs Pinkerton . . .

(MUTTSY and DR BARK disappear)

NARRATOR: *(Strumming a chord or two)*: Hey, Muttsy. How did it go?

MUTTSY: *(Reappearing)*: Oh, it was great!

ACTOR 2: Dr Bark put you right, eh?

MUTTSY: Mrs Pinkerton put me right.

ACTOR 3: Who's Mrs Pinkerton?

MUTTSY: She is the most gorgeous lady in the whole wide world. She runs the Dog Day Dating Service.

NARRATOR: I didn't know there was a Dog Day Dating Service. Did you know there was a Dog Day Dating Service?

ACTORS: Nope!

MUTTSY: Well there is. Mrs Pinkerton wrote down all my details on her computer. Height. Hair colour. Profession. Hobbies . . .

ACTOR 1: You did remember to tell her you're a dog . . . ?

MUTTSY: Yeah, she was very particular about that. 'We've got the ideal partner for you,' she said. Those were her very words: 'Ideal partner'.

ACTOR 2: And when are you going to meet your 'Ideal partner', Muttsy?

MUTTSY: Tonight. Mrs Pinkerton's coming round to introduce us. *(He sighs)*: I wonder what her name is . . .

ACTOR 3: Rover.

ACTOR 4: Bonzo.

ACTOR 2: Chi Chi.

MUTTSY: Stop making fun of me!

NARRATOR: Okay, Muttsy. What do *you* think her name is?

MUTTSY: I think it's . . . Jeanie.

NARRATOR, ACTORS: Jeanie!

MUTTSY: Yeah. You know, like in the song.

NARRATOR: Ah – the song about Jeanie with the light brown hair? *(To the ACTORS)*: I think we ought to sing it, don't you?

ACTOR 4: Just give us a note.

(The NARRATOR strums the chord, and they start to sing, MUTTSY looking on)

NARRATOR, ACTORS:

I dream of Jeanie with the light brown hair,
Borne, like a zephyr, on the summer air,
I see her tripping where the bright streams play,
Happy are the daisies that dance on her way.
Many were the wild notes her merry voice would pour,
Many were the blithe birds that warbled them o'er.
Ah, I dream of Jeanie with the light brown hair,
Floating like a zephyr on the soft summer air.

MUTTSY: Excuse me – that's very nice, but I'd like to have it more doggified.

NARRATOR: Whatever you want, Muttsy.

NARRATOR, ACTORS:

I dream of Jeanie with the light brown fur,
A cross between a bulldog and a Yorkshire terrier
I see her sniffing where the bright streams play,
Happy are the other dogs that dance on her way.
Many were the wild notes her merry voice would pour (ho-o-owl!)
Many were the alley cats that warbled them o'er.
Ah, I dream of Jeanie with the light brown fur,
A cross between a bulldog and a Yorkshire terrier

(MUTTSY sighs, and falls into a reverie. MRS PINKERTON stands)

PINKERTON: Hello! Mr Muttsy Dog?

MUTTSY: Mrs Pinkerton!

PINKERTON: *(As though waiting at the door)*: May I come in?

MUTTSY: Yes, yes. Oh, Mrs Pinkerton, you look ravishing today.

PINKERTON: Why, thank you, Muttsy.

MUTTSY: Do sit down . . .

(PINKERTON sits on the empty chair)

Well? Have you brought her?

PINKERTON: I know you're going to be thrilled Muttsy. You two are going to be so happy together!

MUTTSY: Could you tell me her name . . . ?

PINKERTON: Of course – it's Jeanie.

MUTTSY: Jeanie! I can't believe it! Oh, Jeanie, my first girl friend!

PINKERTON: *(Reaching into her bag)*: Come on, Jeanie. Time to meet Muttsy.

(She produces a bone, and sets it up on stage next to MUTTSY)

There we are!

(Laughter and whistles from the ACTORS. MUTTSY gawps at the bone)

Isn't she your type, Muttsy?

MUTTSY: Oh – yes, yes, of course she is. I'm just having first date nerves.

PINKERTON: I understand. It takes a little time to get used to someone new. Maybe I should leave you two alone together?

MUTTSY: Er, yeah . . .

PINKERTON: *(Getting to her feet)*: On behalf of the Dog Day Dating Service may I extend our best wishes for a blossoming romance!

MUTTSY: Yeah. Thanks, Mrs Pinkerton.

PINKERTON: Bye, Muttsy.

(She resumes her place. MUTTSY looks at the bone and clears his throat hoarsely)

MUTTSY: Well, hi . . . You'll have to excuse me – I get bashful at times like this . . . Sort of tongue tied . . . Same for you, eh? . . . Yeah.

(He looks around the room)

Would you like to take a walk? There's a real good lamppost down the road . . . You don't want to take a walk? . . . Okay, then. That's fine. *(In sudden panic, throwing his head back)*: What am I doing? Why me, Lord? Why does this happen to me?

NARRATOR: What's up now, Muttsy?

MUTTSY: It's all gone disastrously wrong. I need help. I'm on the verge of a breakdown.

ACTOR 4: What do you want us to do?

MUTTSY: Call Dr Bark. Quick.

ACTOR 1: You want an appointment?

MUTTSY: No, I'm too far gone for that. Get him to make a house call.

ACTOR 3: Just like that, with a snap of the fingers?

MUTTSY: Yeah, just like that.

NARRATOR: Okay, everyone. One, two three –

NARRATOR, ACTORS: SNAP!

(DR BARK appears)

DR BARK: Next!

MUTTSY: Oh, Doc! Boy, am I glad to see you!

DR BARK: Something up?

MUTTSY: This Mrs Pinkerton you sent me to. She's matched me with the wrong person.

DR BARK: The wrong person!

MUTTSY: Just take a look.

DR BARK: *(Looking at the bone)*: Hm. She's a bit on the skinny side, it's true.

MUTTSY: Skinny! I've seen more meat on a knitting needle!

DR BARK: Have you tried feeding her fudgecake and chip butties?

MUTTSY: Oh, come on, Doc. There must be something you can do.

DR BARK: Well, actually there is. I call it my 'bone improvement scheme'. Music!

NARRATOR: Right here.

DR BARK: Now what sort of bone is she?

MUTTSY: I dunno. A toe bone, I'd say. *(To the ACTORS)*: What do you think?

NARRATOR, ACTORS: Yeah. Definitely. A toe bone.

DR BARK: Well that's as good a place to start as any.

(A simple version of ***Dem Bones*** *is sung. (*) indicates a single handclap*

from the ACTORS, who can also perform the following actions on the chorus)

(THE DANCE): (The first three lines consist of hand actions only and are identical. For the first 'bones' have the right arm lifted as though to shake the fist, with the upper arm horizontal and the forearm vertical. On the beat of 'bones' slap the lower outside of the forearm with the left hand. Reverse arms for the second 'bones'. Punch the fists together (not too hard!) on the beat before 'dry', and on the third 'bones' point them outwards emphatically with the index fingers of both hands:

Dem bones, dem bones, dem (*) dry bones,

During the 'Now' of the final line bend the knees forward, slapping them with the hands on 'hear'. Flex, and slap the chest on 'word', then on 'Lord' throw both arms straight up in the air, shaking the fingers:

Now hear the word of the Lord!)

NARRATOR, BARK: *Well the toe bone's connected to the foot bone*
And the foot bone's connected to the leg bone
And the leg bone's connected to the knee bone
Now hear the word of the Lord!

EVERYONE: *Dem bones, dem bones, dem dry bones,*
Dem bones, dem bones, dem dry bones,

Dem bones, dem bones, dem dry bones,
Now hear the word of the Lord!

NARRATOR, BARK: *The knee bone's connected to the (*) thigh bone,*
And the thigh bone's connected to the (*) hip bone,
And the hip bone's connected to the (*) back bone,
Now hear the word of the Lord!

EVERYONE: *Dem bones, dem bones, dem dry bones,*
Dem bones, dem bones, dem dry bones,
Dem bones, dem bones, dem dry bones,
Now hear the word of the Lord!

NARRATOR, BARK: *The back bone's connected to the*
ACTORS: *(*) collar bone,*

NARRATOR, BARK: *And the collar bone's connected to the*

ACTORS: *(*) neck bone*

NARRATOR, BARK: *And the neck bone's connected to the*

ACTORS: *(*) head bone,*

EVERYONE: *Now hear the word of the Lord!*

Dem bones, dem bones, dem dry bones,
Dem bones, dem bones, dem dry bones,
Dem bones, dem bones, dem dry bones,
Now hear the word of the Lord!

(At the end of the song the bone is removed and JEANIE appears)

MUTTSY: Jeanie!

JEANIE: Muttsy!

MUTTSY: To think – I've been waiting for you all these years.

JEANIE: And I for you.

MUTTSY: And now, at last, we're together.

JEANIE: Say you'll never leave me.

MUTTSY: I'll never leave you.

JEANIE: Oh Muttsy!

MUTTSY: Marry me, Jeanie.

JEANIE: Do you mean that, Muttsy?

MUTTSY: With all my heart, Jeanie.

JEANIE: Oh darling!

MUTTSY: Oh sweetheart!

(They kiss)

NARRATOR, ACTORS: Aaaaaah!

MUTTSY: Boy, Jeanie, you sure know how to teach an old dog new tricks.

JEANIE: Well, Muttsy, you're my prime pal.

MUTTSY: When you think about it, we've got a lot in common.

JEANIE: Fleas.

MUTTSY: Yeah. Stuff like that. What's your favourite colour, Jeanie?

JEANIE: Brown.

MUTTSY: Mine too! What about your favourite TV show?

JEANIE: One dog and his man.

MUTTSY: Yeah! Oh, Jeanie, I'm so in love with

you I could tear the trousers off a postman.

JEANIE: And just think – we might never have found each other.

MUTTSY: If it weren't for Mrs Pinkerton and the Doc.

(They sigh and lean against each other for a moment, in silence)

JEANIE: Hey, Muttsy, will you do something for me?

MUTTSY: You know I'd do anything for you, Jeanie.

JEANIE: It's nothing much.

MUTTSY: Just tell me. I'll do it.

JEANIE: It's just that I'm . . .

MUTTSY: Yeah?

JEANIE: Completely crazy about . . .

MUTTSY: Yeah?

JEANIE: Discos.

NARRATOR, ACTORS: Discos!

MUTTSY: *(Faltering)*: Discos?

JEANIE: Yeah. You know. Bopdoowop discos. I love them. I couldn't live without going to a disco at least twice a week.

NARRATOR, ACTORS: Twice a week!

MUTTSY: *(Faltering even more)*: Twice a week!

ACTOR 4: Hee hee hee!

MUTTSY: Shut up!

JEANIE: What's the matter, Muttsy?

MUTTSY: I hate discos!

JEANIE: What?

MUTTSY: I hate discos. They give me a headache. They make my ears curl and my teeth fall out!

(More cardboard teeth are thrown over the screen)

JEANIE: *(Wounded)*: You don't mean that!

MUTTSY: I certainly do. In my opinion there is nothing so base, so detestable, so utterly loathsome as a disco!

JEANIE: *(Withdrawing)*: Oh! You beast!

MUTTSY: Jeanie!

JEANIE: Take your paws off me!

MUTTSY: But it's only discos I hate. I love tea dances. Jumble sales. Whist drives . . .

JEANIE: Go away, I don't ever want to see you again!

MUTTSY: But Jeanie . . . !

(She leaves, and there is a ghastly pause)

MUTTSY: *(With a sigh to the audience)*: Oh boy, it's a dog's life. I should have settled for the bone . . .

(The ACTORS shake their heads sympathetically)

ACTOR 1: Oh dear, you really messed it up, Muttsy.

MUTTSY: It's my fate. You see? I was right. Everybody hates me. *(Looking skyward)*: Why me, Lord?

HOUND OF HEAVEN: *(In suitably sonorous tones)*: Because you're a twit. That's why.

(NARRATOR and ACTORS look around to see who spoke)

MUTTSY: *(To ACTOR 1)*: Did you say that?

ACTOR 1 Wasn't me.

MUTTSY: Who are you?

HOUND OF HEAVEN: I am the Hound of Heaven. And I've come to have a little talk with you.

MUTTSY: It's the Hound of Heaven! God's right hand dog, with the snow white collar! *(Looking upward)*: I'm sorry, Mr Hound, sir. You were saying?

HOUND OF HEAVEN: It's not becoming for a dog to be a twit, Muttsy. 'Everybody hates me.' What nonsense!

MUTTSY: But it's true.

HOUND OF HEAVEN: Any more of that and I'll put you in doghouse. You're lucky Muttsy. Most dogs only have one human friend. You've got lots of them. And they'll even take you to discos.

MUTTSY: But I hate discos! They give me a headache. They make my ears curl and my teeth fall out!

(More cardboard teeth are thrown over the screen)

HOUND OF HEAVEN: That's a fib. You hate discos because you can't dance!

MUTTSY: I don't have the figure for it. And I'd have to get all dressed up like a dog's dinner . . .

ACTOR 4: Go on, Muttsy. Try dancing. You'll enjoy it.

HOUND OF HEAVEN: She's right, Muttsy.

MUTTSY: Do I have to?

HOUND OF HEAVEN: Yes.

MUTTSY: Right now?

NARRATOR, ACTORS: Yes!

MUTTSY: Oh all right, then. I'll try it.

(Cheers and applause from the NARRATOR and ACTORS, who stand up to sing and dance the closing song. Half way through the song MUTTSY is joined again by JEANIE, and also by DR BARK. At the end MUTTSY and JEANIE kiss)

Trouble in Zingzang

Characters: at least 6
Performance time: 5 minutes

Written for under-11s and based loosely on the parable of the vineyards, TROUBLE IN ZINGZANG can be performed easily with as many as thirty children – provided you impose the discipline of careful rehearsal and keep the beating up of the MINISTER from turning into a mass physical assault. Other tips: remember to use a large umbrella, to get the 'Boo!' and 'No!' short and sharp, and to use some imagination in the casting – ZANG is male character, but I suspect the drama will have more educational value if he's played by a girl.

(The ZINGERS stand closely packed to stage right; the two READERS side by side, stage left. All face the audience)

READER ONE: Not so long ago,

READER TWO: in a place not so far away,

READER ONE: there was a country called Zingzang, ruled by a man called General Zang.

(ZANG enters to a general round of applause, which stops abruptly when he raises his arms. He then stamps, and stands in a salute, facing the audience)

READER TWO: General Zang was a good person. His laws were fair, and the country of Zingzang prospered.

READER ONE: But like most Generals, General Zang had problems. The people of Zingzang, called the Zingers, thought he was wet.

PEOPLE: Boo!

(At this ZANG breaks the salute, turns to his right, puts his hands on his hips, and frowns at the ZINGERS)

READER TWO: And other generals in other countries thought that Zingzang should be ruled by *them*.

READER ONE: Invasion!

(ZING turns full circle and peers into the distance stage left, trying to see the enemy. The MINISTER comes on from stage right with a raincoat and a suitcase)

READER TWO: And so it was that General Zang had to fight to save Zingzang from the enemy.

(The MINISTER touches ZANG's shoulder. During the following sequence ZANG turns, looks at his watch, and allows the

MINISTER to help him on with the coat)

READER ONE: And were the Zingers sad?

PEOPLE: No!

READER TWO: Were they afraid?

PEOPLE: No!

READER ONE: Didn't they cry?

PEOPLE: No!

READER TWO: Then what *did* they do?

(By now ZANG has donned the coat and picked up the case. He escorts the MINISTER off, stage left. At this point – immediately after READER TWO's question – the ZINGERS make faces and blow raspberries)

READER ONE: Now among the Zingers was a man called Itchipox.

(ITCHIPOX pushes forward to stand in front of the ZINGERS. He is wearing tasteless shades and carrying a ghettoblaster)

ITCHIPOX: Aha!

READER TWO: Itchipox thought he was a regular king of the Zingers, and when General Zang went to war Itchipox thought they'd seen the last of him. So he said:

ITCHIPOX: *(Flinging his arms up)*: Let's have a party!

(Immediately ITCHIPOX switches on a tape of loud rock music. For about five seconds the ZINGERS dance wildly. But then ITCHIPOX suddenly switches the tape off, and stands, uncertainly, with one hand over his mouth. The other ZINGERS watch him)

READER TWO: But then he had a thought . . .

READER ONE: That special time of year had come when the Zingers had to give something to General Zang.

READER TWO: Remember what that is, Itchipox?

ITCHIPOX: Er . . .

READER ONE: It's not a birthday present.

READER TWO: And it's not a kick in the ankle.

READER ONE: It's taxes.

ITCHIPOX: What?

ZINGERS: Taxes!

READER TWO: Were they pleased?

ZINGERS: *(Led by ITCHIPOX)*: No!

READER ONE: Weren't they even just a little weenie bit pleased?

ZINGERS: No!

READER TWO: Then what *did* they think about it?

ZINGERS: Boo!

(The MINISTER enters from stage left. He is now wearing a hat; he carries an open umbrella and a bag containing a soft shoe and an old shirt. He pauses in the space between the ZINGERS and the READERS, and looks around as though surveying the scenery)

READER ONE: *(As the MINISTER enters)*: So when the taxman came they didn't pay their taxes. Instead, they beat him up!

MINISTER: *(Suddenly seeing the ZINGERS)*: Help!

(The MINISTER drops to his knees, pulling the umbrella down to screen him from the audience. Led forward by ITCHIPOX – who places the ghettoblaster carefully behind the umbrella – the ZINGERS close in from the back until they form a tight semi-circle behind the MINISTER. Starting with ITCHIPOX, each of the ZINGERS now starts to yell repeatedly one of the words below)

ITCHIPOX: Biff!

ZINGERS: Bang! Smack! Growl! Boot! Ow! Eek! Ooh!

(As the shouting starts the MINISTER opens his bag and tosses into the air the hat, then the shoe, then the shirt. When the last item has been tossed out the TAXMAN lies down behind the umbrella. ITCHIPOX then jumps to his feet, facing stage left. At his cry all the ZINGERS freeze)

ITCHIPOX: Wait!

READER TWO: Zingzang is like our world.

READER ONE: And General Zang is like God,

READER TWO: and the Zingers are like *us*.

READER ONE: We don't live the way God wants us to.

READER TWO: We're selfish and unkind.

READER ONE: And that's not good enough!

READER TWO: And you know why not?

READER ONE: Because one day God's going to come back, and then he'll want to know what we've been up to.

ITCHIPOX: *(Unfreezing, pointing off stage left)*: Look out! It's General Zang!

(The ZINGERS unfreeze, draw back from the MINISTER, and hurriedly

retreat to their previous position, stage right. At the same time ZANG enters from stage left, pausing stage left of the MINISTER, who is now lying behind the umbrella. Without looking down, ZANG puts his hands on his hips)

ZANG: Where's my Minister?

READER TWO: said General Zang.

ITCHIPOX: *(Arms outspread and smiling)*: On holiday!

READER ONE: said Itchipox.

ZANG: *(Pointing at the MINISTER)*: And what's this, lying on the floor?

READER TWO: said General Zang.

ITCHIPOX: *(Bending forward to look closely)*: Just an umbrella!

READER ONE: said Itchipox.

ZANG: *(Grimly, bending down and snatching up the umbrella)*: It's a body!

READER TWO: said General Zang.

ITCHIPOX: *(Indicating smallness with thumb and index finger)*: Only a small one!

READER ONE: said Itchipox.

ZANG: *(Taking down the umbrella and waving it at ITCHIPOX)*: It's my Minister, isn't it?

READER TWO: said General Zang.

ZINGERS: *(Putting their hands to their cheeks and looking guilty)*: Whoops!

READER ONE: said the Zingers.

(The Zingers hold pose. ZANG turns his back on them and angrily flings down the umbrella)

READER TWO: Then the king was very angry, because his people had done something wicked and wrong.

READER ONE: But he decided to give the Zingers another chance. So he said:

ZANG: *(Turning back to the ZINGERS)*: Anyone who's sorry, come over here with me!

(In response, all the ZINGERS except ITCHIPOX cross cautiously behind the MINISTER, as you might cross a room with a cobra in the middle of it, and sit down by ZANG)

And anyone who's not sorry – *(Pointing sharply)*: get out of my country!

(ITCHIPOX jumps, and dashes off, stage right. ZANG starts to help the ZINGERS to their feet)

READER TWO: And that's the story of how General Zang came back to the Zingers.

READER ONE: And the Zingers came back to him.

(Finally ZANG reaches down and touches the MINISTER, who stands)

READER TWO: And how,

READER ONE: in the end,

READER TWO: everyzing zanged in Zingzang.

(ZANG, the MINISTER, and the ZINGERS all take a bow)

Yes

Characters: 2
Performance time: 3 minutes

A lot of marriages begin with a fanfare and end in a dirge. Nearer to the dirge end is a phase characterized – and probably preserved – by habit. Wrote William Morris of love: 'The void shall not weary, the fear shall not alter/These lips and these eyes of the loved and the lover'. Ah, well.

(On the stage area are two comfortable chairs, arranged as in a living room, with a small table between bearing two cups and saucers. THE WIFE is sitting in one of the chairs, staring at her wristwatch)

THE WIFE: Four fifty-nine and fifty-seven seconds. Four fifty-nine and fifty-eight seconds. Four fifty-nine and fifty-nine seconds. Five o'clock.

THE HUSBAND: *(Offstage)*: Home!

THE WIFE: The human chronometer. They should use him to measure the lifespan of quarks.

(THE HUSBAND enters, carrying a newspaper, a magazine, a briefcase and an umbrella)

THE HUSBAND: Hello darling.

THE WIFE: Hello darling.

(THE HUSBAND puts the case and umbrella behind a chair, and unfolds the newspaper and magazine as he moves to the front)

(As he does so): And now I say something creative and polite like 'Nice day at the office?' 'Yes. Nice day in the kitchen?' 'Yes. Tea?' 'Yes.' 'By the way somebody dropped a small thermonuclear device on the greenhouse.' Yes. Yes. Yes.

(By now THE HUSBAND has come around to the front of the furniture and is holding out the magazine to THE WIFE)

Oh, but it's Friday, and here's my copy of *Charwoman's Weekly*. Darling, what a nice surprise!

(She takes the magazine. They give each other a perfunctory smile, and then sit)

That means we can spread out, relax, and get down to the *serious* business of: communicating.

(They turn away from one another, decisively opening the magazine and newspaper. THE HUSBAND *proceeds to drink his tea)*

THE HUSBAND: I see the FT index is down again.

THE WIFE: Adverts for depilatory cream.

THE HUSBAND: Another takeover's gone to the Monopolies Commission.

THE WIFE: Interesting things to do with tinned peaches.

THE HUSBAND: Spurs lost, too.

THE WIFE: Dear Marjorie, my boyfriend is a twenty-five stone greasy slob. Should I marry him?

(She throws the magazine over her shoulder. THE HUSBAND *sticks his cup out without lowering the newspaper.* THE WIFE *duly fills it from the pot, then leans forward to the audience)*

Dear Marjorie, I used to have a marriage. Now I have a timetable with legs on. It consumes tea, and creates laundry, but otherwise serves no useful purpose. Please tell me what to do with it. Yours sincerely, Cracking Up. *(Pause)*: Dear Cracking Up, my advice to you is twofold. First, change your name. Second, do your utmost to rekindle the spark and spontaneity of youth! Where is the young tigress he married? Where is the passion he once saw in your eyes? Where is the sheer, raw power of the female spirit?

THE HUSBAND: Did you say something?

THE WIFE: *(Interrupted, but now vampishly slicking back her hair)*: Yes. Darling . . .

THE HUSBAND: What?

THE WIFE: I've been thinking.

THE HUSBAND: *(Dropping his newspaper to look at her)*: Thinking?

THE WIFE: Why don't we go away? Together. You and me. A sort of second honeymoon.

(She gets up and draws him to his feet. She holding him close, they waltz slowly, turning a half circle between each line)

Don't you remember – the sunset over the Mediterranean?

THE HUSBAND: I remember those pesky flies.

THE WIFE: The candlelit dinners.

THE HUSBAND: The diarrhoea.

THE WIFE: The long evenings spent dancing under the stars.

THE HUSBAND: The cockroaches in the bed.

THE WIFE: *(She stops dancing and pulls his face close to hers)*: We could – rediscover one another!

(A pause. THE HUSBAND breaks free, sits again and picks up his newspaper)

THE WIFE: Well?

THE HUSBAND: Rediscover one another? What do you mean – rediscover one another?

THE WIFE: Darling, we've been married twenty years, and you hardly know me.

THE HUSBAND: Rubbish. Of course I know you.

THE WIFE: Not the important things about me.

THE HUSBAND: The important things about you are, one, you can cook, two, you can clean a house, and three, you can bring up children. That's it.

THE WIFE: Well if all you want out of marriage is food, babies and clean carpets, why didn't you marry a housekeeper?

THE HUSBAND: I did. Stop going on about it.

(THE WIFE sits, looking away)

THE WIFE: And now I say something peaceable and submissive, like 'Yes, you're right. You're always right.' He won't hear me. And I'll collect the cups and do what I am expected to do, not because I wish to, but because it is easy. Yes. Yes. Yes. And though I speak, I shall not say another word.

(THE HUSBAND suddenly looks at his watch and folds his newspaper)

THE HUSBAND: Six o'clock, darling.

THE WIFE: Oh! Dinner time already?

THE HUSBAND: Television till nine, then bed.

THE WIFE: What a cosy life we lead.

THE HUSBAND: *(Making a very weak effort at rising from the chair)*: Can I help you with . . . ?

THE WIFE: No, you just stay right where you are. You've had a hard day, so you put up your feet and watch the news. Making dinner! *(Laying her hand on his)*: That's not your job – is it, darling?

Herod Sees the Shrink

Characters: 2
Performance time: 4 minutes

This sketch, a gloss on the familiar story of the Magi, pictures the old tyrant consulting his psychoanalyst. Making the most of the humour depends on creating the right tension between the characters. Each plays on the other's weakness: HEROD on SIGMUND's covert and bizarre hobby of hypnotizing chickens, SIGMUND on HEROD's passion to understand his dreams. Being king, of course, HEROD has the upper hand. Or does he?

(A comfortable chair, suggestive of a throne, is placed centre stage, with a small stool to its left. HEROD makes an entrance, and perches on the edge of the chair in a baronial pose)

HEROD: Sigmund! . . . Sig-*mund!*

SIGMUND: *(Loudly, off)*: Just a minute, Your Majesty . . .

HEROD: Sigmund, the cook has lodged another complaint.

SIGMUND: *(Still off)*: Oh?

HEROD: Someone's been hypnotizing the chickens again.

(A pause as HEROD waits for a reply)

Sigmund?

SIGMUND: *(Still off)*: Yes, Your Majesty?

HEROD: It wasn't you or one of your little friends, was it, Sigmund?

SIGMUND: *(Still off)*: No! No, we didn't do it.

(A sound suspiciously like that of a chicken being hypnotized is heard offstage, followed by a thud)

HEROD: *(Cocking his ear and giving a sly laugh)*: Good. People interfering with the Imperial chickens are liable to have their entrails displayed in the Imperial Museum . . .

(But SIGMUND has hurried on stage and is standing just in front of the stool. He is brushing his sleeves frantically. His hair is dishevelled, his collar open, his white lab coat incorrectly buttoned. He is panting)

Ah, there you are.

(Herod regards him. There is a pause)

Aren't you forgetting something, Sigmund?

SIGMUND: Forgetting something?

HEROD: My bit of positive feedback.

SIGMUND: Oh! *(He kneels hastily, side on to the audience but facing HEROD, and does lavish obeisance)*: Mighty Herod, Herod the Great, Herod the Intelligent, Sophisticated, Tasteful and Spectacular. Herod the . . . er . .

HEROD: Salubrious. (*When SIGMUND fails to respond*): Salubrious!

SIGMUND: Oh. Herod the Salubrious and . . . er . . .

HEROD: *(Wearily)*: Never mind. Stand up.

(SIGMUND stands, HEROD looks up at him)

Sit down!

(SIGMUND sits on the stool. HEROD slaps his knees and stands)

Now, Sigmund. I have a small problem. Get your notebook out and record it.

SIGMUND: Of course, Your Majesty.

(SIGMUND fishes in his pocket and pulls out the notebook in a cloud of feathers. He casts a swift, anxious glance at HEROD, but HEROD has his back to him and takes no notice)

HEROD: Sometimes I think . . . sometimes I think I'm *not* the most important person in the world.

SIGMUND: *(Furiously stuffing the feathers back in his pocket)*: Oh, Your Majesty –

HEROD: It's foolish, I know. A big, grown-up tyrant like me. But – I keep having this nightmare. You're good with nightmares, aren't you, Sigmund?

(He turns as he addresses the question. SIGMUND finishes with the feathers just in time)

SIGMUND: Yes, I have them every day.

HEROD: Splendid. Then this one will pose you no difficulty.

(He beckons to SIGMUND, who stands and steps forward. HEROD puts an arm around his shoulder and stretches the other one out to define a distant horizon somewhere beyond the audience)

Imagine . . . a desert at sunsest.

SIGMUND: Yes.

HEROD: I am surveying my dominions when, suddenly, out of the East, come three Wise Men, bearing gifts. 'Herod!' they cry. 'Where is the King of the Jews?' 'Look no further,' say I. 'He is standing before you.'

SIGMUND: What then?

HEROD: Then they look at me and say – 'Where?' 'Here. Me, I'm the King of the Jews,' I reply. And then one of them laughs. He *laughs*! 'Oh, no,' he says. 'Oh, no. There must be a mistake. The King of the Jews *we're* looking for is a baby. See! There is his star!'

(HEROD points.
SIGMUND peers into the distance)

SIGMUND: Where?

HEROD: No, you ninkumpoop! It's in the dream.

SIGMUND: And then?

HEROD: Well, that's it. Over.

SIGMUND: No two mile fall from a clifftop? No attack by a vampire bunny?

HEROD: Don't toy with me, Sigmund. I'm sick.

SIGMUND: Yes. Well, you ought to see a doctor. If you'll excuse me . . .

(SIGMUND makes to leave, but HEROD, who still has his arm around him, clutches him by the collar and pulls him back. He holds SIGMUND's face close to his own)

HEROD: You *are* a doctor, you wimp. And if you don't come up with a successful treatment I shall see to it personally that you're sent to the kitchen and plucked. Do we understand one another?

SIGMUND: *(In a strangled voice)*: Yes, Your Majesty . . .

HEROD: Good.

(HEROD pushes SIGMUND back on to the stool and sits on the chair)

SIGMUND: What do you want to know?

HEROD: The meaning of the dream.

SIGMUND: There are two. Which do you want – the sensible one or the silly one?

HEROD: I don't care.

SIGMUND: All right. It occurs to me that these three Wise Men you mention may represent a latent mother-fixation, and the baby-king your unrealized desire to return to childhood. All of which would indicate that you are a perfectly normal, rational human being . . .

HEROD: Wonderful.

SIGMUND: *(Levelly – with a little malicious pleasure)*: That's the silly explanation.

HEROD: *(His face falls. Grimly, after a pause)*: Go on.

SIGMUND: More likely, you have mental disorder common to tyrants of your age and brutality, called Phobia de la Military Coup.

HEROD: And what's the cure?

SIGMUND: Abdication.

(HEROD glowers at him. SIGMUND sobers fast)

That was a joke.

HEROD: Get back to the chicken run, Sigmund.

SIGMUND: *(Rising)*: Your Majesty.

(He starts to leave)

HEROD: *(Calling after SIGMUND)*: One more thing . . . this kind of nightmare doesn't come true, does it?

SIGMUND: *(Unctiously)*: There is no record of such an occurrence, Your Majesty.

(SIGMUND exits. HEROD nods to himself, reassured)

HEROD: Good. Don't want my Christmas spoiled by an insurrection. Well . . . *(He gets up briskly)*: an evening stroll in the desert, a last look at my kingdoms as the sun goes down. *(Leaving)*: And then I shall sleep the sleep of the just . . .

A Family Photo

Characters: 9 adults, 5 children
Performance time: 5 minutes

Although the family is a far more important social unit than its critics realize, it has to be said that family life is, for many people, a mixed blessing. There are times when members even of the best families feel like clouting one another; and in any family there can be individuals who push the traditional values of love and loyalty close to breaking point. This sketch is not meant either to vilify or idealize the family, only to explore it in one of its many different forms.

(The BRIDE, the GROOM and the FAMILY troop on stage and assemble as though for a wedding photograph. The CHILDREN squat down at the front. Behind them, stage left to stage right, are BIG SIS (seated), the BRIDE and GROOM (standing), and GRANDPA and GRANDMA (seated). For most of the sketch the BRIDE and GROOM pose together like waxworks, looking out at the audience. Behind BIG SIS stand MOTHER and FATHER and GREAT AUNT

NORA. Behind GRANDPA and GRANDMA stand UNCLE SID, BELINDA, and later DENZIL. There is some effort involved in getting GRANDPA seated. At first DENZIL hangs back stage right, looking over his shoulder)

MOTHER: *(Presiding, as they come on stage)*: Quickly, quickly. One with everybody together. The whole family. Denzil, that includes you . . .

DENZIL: Oh mum!

MOTHER: Don't be awkward, Denzil. *(To FATHER)*: Darling, tell him to come here.

FATHER: Er . . . please, Denzil, don't get your mother upset.

MOTHER: Do it, Denzil!

DENZIL: *(Looking back)*: Can't Fiona be in the photo?

MOTHER: No.

DENZIL: Why not?

MOTHER: She's not family, is she?

DENZIL: She will be.

MOTHER: *(With a withering gaze off stage right)*: Not if I have anything to do with it, she won't. Dreadful girl. Now come on, Denzil. We're waiting.

(DENZIL reluctantly takes his place)

Okay, everyone. Backs straight. Big smiles . . .

(They all freeze, chests out, holding their breath and grinning inanely into the audience. There is a short pause)

UNCLE SID: *(Through his grin)*: What's the hitch?

BELINDA: I think his flash unit's broken.

DENZIL: He's changing the film.

(They all release their breath and sag. GRANDMA sighs and gets out her knitting; BIG SIS starts to preen the cuddly toy she is holding; DENZIL inspects his fingernails; BELINDA combs her hair; FATHER looks around nervously)

GREAT AUNT NORA: *(To MOTHER)*: Oh Daphne, this is the end. And just after we'd got Grandpa sitting down.

UNCLE SID: *(To GRANDPA)*: Are you comfy, Colonel?

GREAT AUNT NORA: Don't start him, Sidney.

GRANDPA: What?

UNCLE SID: How's – the – war – going?

GRANDPA: Oh, the war! The war's splendid. Just back from Khartoum. Had quite a dust up with the Zulus, I can tell you.

GRANDMA: Not now, dear.

GRANDPA: What?

GRANDMA: I'm trying to do my knitting!

BELINDA: The war's over, Grandpa.

GRANDPA: Over? Rubbish! The war's never over.

BELINDA: *(Leaning forward, putting her comb away)*: It's been over for seventy years!

GRANDPA: *(To GRANDMA)*: Florence, is that true?

MOTHER: No, it's not. Not here, at any rate. *(She casts a warning glance at BELINDA)*: Stanley, just make sure everyone's here, will you?

(Appeased, GRANDPA settles down for a doze. BELINDA is scowling. FATHER points to members of the party)

FATHER: Er . . . right. You, me, Grandpa, Grandma, Uncle Sid, Great Aunt Nora, er . . .

UNCLE SID: Speed it up, Stan. We want to be away before closing time.

GREAT AUNT NORA: Sidney!

FATHER: Ah . . . Belinda, Denzil, and Denzil's . . . ?

DENZIL: Fiancée.

MOTHER: Friend.

UNCLE SID: Bit of stuff.

BELINDA: *(Giving UNCLE SID a shove)*: Oh – you're so sexist, you are!

MOTHER: *(To BELINDA)*: Now, now.

DENZIL: It's all right. She's not here, anyway.

FATHER: And, er . . . Big Sis . . .

MOTHER: She *is* your daughter, darling.

FATHER: Yes. Of course. Big Daughter. Plus *four* children . . . ?

BIG SIS: Five, Dad.

UNCLE SID: Cor! Have you had another one while we weren't looking, Sis?

BIG SIS: 'Niece' to you, Sid.

FATHER: Well we'd better check. Er . . . hands up, how many of you down there are Sis's children?

CHILDREN: *(Holding their hands up enthusiastically)*: Me me me me me me! *(They stop when GRANDPA speaks)*

GRANDPA: *(Awoken, struggling to his feet)*: Zulus!

BELINDA: *(Restraining him)*: It's not the Zulus, Grandpa. It's Sis's kids.

UNCLE SID: Easy mistake to make.

BELINDA: *(Settling him)*: Sit down, Grandpa.

GRANDMA: *(To everyone in general)*: I haven't seen Sis's husband here this afternoon.

BIG SIS: That's 'cause Reggie and me aren't speaking.

GREAT AUNT NORA: Not speaking! How long has this been going on?

MOTHER: It's nothing. Just a lovers' tiff.

BIG SIS: We always have an argument round Saturday lunch. That way Reggie has an excuse to go down the football with his mates.

GREAT AUNT NORA: Daphne!

MOTHER: She's exaggerating. *(Icily, to BIG SIS)*: Reggie's away on a weekend business trip, isn't he, Sis?

BIG SIS: Is he? Never told me.

MOTHER: In Spain. Otherwise he'd have come *wouldn't* he, Sis?

DENZIL: I thought Reggie was a park attendant –

MOTHER: *Denzil!* Now – are we all ready?

FAMILY: Ready!

MOTHER: What are we?

FAMILY: Family!

GRANDMA: Sticking together through thick and thin.

FATHER: Extended.

DENZIL: Like a broken concertina.

MOTHER: But still able to knock up a good tune. Oh wasn't it grand?

(FATHER gives the note, and the FAMILY start to sing the final two lines of the wedding march. The

GROOM raises the BRIDE's hand as though processing)

FAMILY: *Bah* bah b'*bah, Bah* bah b'*bah!*
Bah bah b'*bah*-bah, b'*bah* bah b'*bah!*

(The FAMILY turn slightly inward to face the BRIDE and GROOM)

MOTHER: Dearly beloved, we were gathered here today to witness the marriage of our Emma to their Norman.

GREAT AUNT NORA: Who gavest this woman to be married to this man?

FATHER: Er . . . I think that was me, wasn't it?

UNCLE SID: Emma Joan Elizabeth Ida Ryan-Fitzpatrick Smith, did you take this man to be your lawfully wedded husband?

THE WOMEN: She did

GREAT AUNT NORA: Norman Ogilvie Erasmus Xerxes Alexander Brown, did you take this woman to be your lawfully wedded wife?

THE MEN: He did.

MOTHER: *(After a pause, indulgently)*: Aren't they a picture? I love weddings! Two young people starting out in life, everything before them . . .

GREAT AUNT NORA: It reminds me of my Arthur. You can't beat a happy marriage. Dear, dear, Arthur . . .

BIG SIS: *(Bleakly)*: That was me ten years ago. Me and Reggie. If only I'd known . . .

(There is a moment's dead silence, and then, simultaneously, MOTHER, GREAT AUNT NORA, and BIG SIS burst loudly into tears. BRIDE and GROOM drop their hands. Everyone faces forward again. GRANDMA thoughtfully picks up her knitting. GRANDPA falls asleep)

MOTHER: *(Sniffing)*: Stanley, give me your handkerchief.

FATHER: (*Producing a handkerchief*): Yes, dear.

MOTHER: Not that one – you've blown your nose on it.

(FATHER hastily produces another, which MOTHER snatches from him with a grimace. GREAT AUNT NORA, MOTHER and BIG SIS are all wiping their eyes)

GRANDMA: So the family goes on. We pass it down, like old silver, from one generation to the next.

(Loud sobs)

I cried, too.

DENZIL: Well I won't be crying.

UNCLE SID: You won't have to. You're a man.

BELINDA: Nor will I!

GRANDMA: Oh . . . you will, dear, you will.

UNCLE SID: All the women in tears. All the men want is a glass of champagne.

GREAT AUNT NORA: *(Recovering)*: Sidney – shame on you!

GRANDMA: Oh, leave him be. It's a special day when we're all together like this, isn't it, Gramps? With the family?

GRANDPA: *(Waking)*: With the what?

FAMILY: The family!

MOTHER: *(Mastering her tears)*: And we're going to enjoy ourselves. Because today we are welcoming a new member.

DENZIL: You mean Big Sis is, you know, again . . .?

BIG SIS: *(Fretfully)*: No, she doesn't. And no, I'm not.

BELINDA: She means Norman.

DENZIL: Norman?

BELINDA: The groom, muttonhead.

DENZIL: Oh, him.

FATHER: *(Pointing forward)*: Er . . . I think the whoeverheis has got the whatsit into the thingummygig . . .

MOTHER: The film into the camera. Thank you, darling. Here we go . . . get ready everyone.

(They all pose again, with serious expressions, not turning as they address the GROOM)

GREAT AUNT NORA: You'll cherish this photograph, Norman.

MOTHER: It's a day to look back on.

BIG SIS: Maybe the only wedding you'll have.

UNCLE SID: And here we all are, Norman.

FATHER: Taking you in.

BELINDA: Helping you out.

MOTHER: Loving.

DENZIL: Hating.

GREAT AUNT NORA: Belonging;

BIG SIS: Muddling along.

GRANDMA: The family. To have and to hold.

FAMILY: Till death us do part!

MOTHER: You may kiss the bride.

(Everyone smiles for the camera as the GROOM kisses the BRIDE. Freeze)

Death and Related Causes

Characters: 4
Performance time: 3 minutes

On a recent episode of TV soap someone uttered the immortal words: 'I value our relationship'. As I recall, the characters had been acquainted for a single afternoon – most of which they had spent in bed together. The remark has an odd connotation: apparently relationships possess a life of their own, quite independent of the people who begin them. One imagines a couple periodically getting their relationship out of its box to tickle it under the chin and watch it run around on the carpet. But what would happen if our relationships really did live in boxes? What awful secrets might be revealed?

(A table is placed diagonally centre stage, facing out past stage left. Behind it sits the DOCTOR, reading his notes. In front, but side-on and facing out past stage right, is an empty chair. A knocking is heard offstage)

DOCTOR: Come in!

(The DOCTOR stands and takes a few paces to stage left to meet his incoming patient. SMITH enters, carrying a hold-all. They shake hands, and the DOCTOR shows SMITH

to the empty seat before resuming his own. SMITH is clearly ailing)

Mr Smith. Do sit down. *(Consulting his notes):* So – you're 28, a mainstream yuppie on ninety thousand a year with two houses, a yacht and a BMW. What's the matter? Going bald? Silk sheets giving you a rash?

(SMITH shakes his head weakly)

Oh, don't tell me you've actually got something *wrong* with you? I thought you people were like Duracell batteries – went on forever.

SMITH: *(Leaning forward, with an effort)*: It's personal, Doctor.

DOCTOR: Personal. Personal. Okay. Well you just make yourself comfy and tell me about it. I mean I've only got fifty acute cases of whooping cough out there in the waiting room, I'm sure I can spare you an hour or two. Don't tell me. I can guess. Relationship trouble . . .

SMITH: *(Feebly)*: Relationship trouble.

DOCTOR: Which one? Wife?

(SMITH nods)

DOCTOR: *(With a sigh)*: All right. Let's see it.

(SMITH reaches into the hold-all and produces a

small cardboard box. He puts it on the table. The DOCTOR opens the lid and looks inside)

Mmm. Certainly looking a bit queasy. Bring any more with you?

SMITH: My relationships at work . . .

DOCTOR: Get them out.

(SMITH delves in the hold-all and starts, mechanically, to put more boxes on the table)

DOCTOR: This been going on long?

SMITH: Quite a while.

(Glancing into another box): Well, it's spreading, that's for sure. *(He leans forward and presses an imaginary intercom)*: Barbara, send in Dr Grimm, will you? *(To SMITH)*: I hope you don't mind. Dr Grimm is more of a specialist in this area . . . these *all* relationships at work?

(SMITH by now has at least seven more boxes on the table. He points out each one individually)

SMITH: Er, no. Children, parents, secretary, neighbours, parrot, gerbil, car . . .

(GRIMM appears, stage left, and approaches the table. SMITH carries on delving)

GRIMM: Hello!

(He comes forward to stand at the end of the table furthest from the audience. The DOCTOR stands to make the introduction)

DOCTOR: Dr Grimm, my patient Mr Smith.

(SMITH interrupts his labours briefly to shake hands with GRIMM. The DOCTOR sits)

GRIMM: So you're having trouble with your relationships.

SMITH: *(Not looking up)*: Yes.

GRIMM: How interesting! And what are these?

SMITH: *(Placing still more boxes on the table and pointing them out)*: My accountant, the political situation, my collection of seventeenth century Japanese blowpipes . . . *(He reaches in for another box)*

GRIMM: *(To the DOCTOR)*: This is highly complex. I think he's developed secondaries. *(Pointing at the intercom)*: Would you mind?

DOCTOR: Not at all.

SMITH: History, Rene Descartes, deconstructivism, the future . . .

GRIMM: *(Half sitting on the table)*: Barbara – would you catch Frank, please? Yes. Suspected relational abnormalities.

DOCTOR: *(Examining the latest boxes)*: They're sick, all right. You don't think this could be terminal?

GRIMM: Your guess is as good as mine on that one.

(FRANK appears, stage left. By now, SMITH has taken out the last and largest of the boxes, and is cuddling it in his lap)

Ah, Frank.

FRANK: *(Coming forward)*: Relationship problems?

GRIMM: Proliferative.

FRANK: *(Stopping just stage left of SMITH, looking down)*: What's he bonding with?

DOCTOR: Just about everything.

FRANK: I see. *(Indicating the large box)*: And this one?

(The DOCTOR and GRIMM shake their heads – they don't know. FRANK reaches down to touch the large box)

Excuse me, young man, may I just take a look?

(SMITH relinquishes the box lamely and sits looking blank)

Oh ho! You have a relationship with your*self*. In fact, quite a *big* relationship with yourself. *(Looking inside)*: Not a pretty sight.

GRIMM: Any idea of the cause, Frank?

FRANK: I'm working on it. Now, Mr ah . . .

DOCTOR: Smith.

FRANK: Mr Smith. Would you like to tell me which one of these is your relationship with God?

SMITH: *(Weakly)*: Who?

GRIMM: God. *(To the DOCTOR)*: That's brilliant. What a diagnostician.

SMITH: *(Getting shakily to his feet)*: God . . . ?

(He gazes around the room, seems about to speak, but suddenly collapses, spreadeagled in the chair)

DOCTOR: Quick. He's arresting!

(There is a burst of manic activity. GRIMM takes SMITH's head in an armlock; the DOCTOR grasps SMITH's left wrist and takes his pulse; FRANK leans over and pounds him four times, rhythmically, on the chest.

SMITH's legs jerk in response, but on the fourth beat they all withdraw and stand up)

FRANK: Too late. We've lost him.

DOCTOR: I suppose it was inevitable.

GRIMM: Given his condition?

DOCTOR: No. Given that it's a Tuesday and I'm the one on morgue duty. And I said I'd be home by five . . .

GRIMM: Mind that dicky back of yours.

(The others watch as the DOCTOR hooks his elbows under SMITH's arms and drags him off backwards, stage left. GRIMM sits in the doctor's chair; FRANK perches on the far end of the table)

GRIMM: Well you were half way there – you got the diagnosis right.

FRANK: It's a common disorder nowadays.

GRIMM: *(Picking over the boxes)*: He had so much . . .

FRANK: Everything but what he most needed.

GRIMM: Is it possible that Mr Smith had no relationship with God?

FRANK: Oh he *had* one, all right. Everybody *has* one. *(He lifts a box and reads the label)*: Here it is.

GRIMM: So what was the problem?

(FRANK opens the box, upturns it, and taps the bottom. It is empty. He shrugs at GRIMM. Freeze)

Good (Evening) News

Characters: 6 principals – including a musician; at least 6 others
Performance time: about 15 minutes

For many Sunday school teachers Christmas brings with it not just a fattening of the proverbial geese but the onerous responsibility of producing the Nativity play. If one or two adults are willing to take part, GOOD (EVENING) NEWS may provide a way out. Although the piece uses a variety of dramatic forms, including music, mime and dance, none of it is especially difficult (if you can walk, you can dance to 'God rest you merry, Gentlemen'), and the whole thing can be staged by as few as a dozen people. No mangers, no barbie dolls playing Jesus. Just a lot of newspapers.

One practical remark on direction. As large casts quickly become unmanageable it's worth making sure that people in the SCENERY – who start the performance lined up at the sides of the stage – are standing in the right order for the dance. Those on each side who will make up the first row of dancers must be placed nearest to the back of the stage, those in the last row nearest to the front.

(The SCENERY lines up on either side of the stage, feet apart, hands behind backs, facing in. JOSEPH is off, stage left; the NEWSVENDOR off, stage right. The NARRATORS stand together extreme stage left, in front of the SCENERY)

NARRATOR 1: Now the birth of Jesus Christ took place this way. When his mother Mary had been betrothed to Joseph, before they came together she was found to be with child of the Holy Spirit . . .

(Enter the NEWSVENDOR to centre stage. He sets up his news-stand, which reads 'Herod boobs again', and stands in front of his chair with an armful of papers)

NEWSVENDOR: *Evening News*! Get your *Evening News*! Herod in top level talks with Roman governors. All in your *Evening News*!

(Enter JOSEPH from stage left)

JOSEPH: *Evening News*, please.

NEWSVENDOR: Thirty pence. And congratulations, Mr Carpenter.

JOSEPH: Congratulations?

NEWSVENDOR: You and the Missus. Can't keep back a story like that, Mr Carpenter. It's all over the town.

JOSEPH: What's all over the town?

NEWSVENDOR: Oh-hoh! You're a wry one, you really are! Soon be hearing the pitter-patter of little mallets, eh? See – there's a photo. 'Bliss of Mary, mum-to-be'.

(He hands the paper to JOSEPH, who examines the front page)

You should've been a Royal, Mr Carpenter.

JOSEPH: 'Baby due in December'! But that's impossible. We only got married in July!

NEWSVENDOR: *(Stopped in his tracks)*: July . . . *(With a swift calculation on his fingers)*: I *see*. Well, that does put a rather different complexion on things, doesn't it?

JOSEPH: Different's not the word for it.

NEWSVENDOR: *(With painful discretion)*: I take it you didn't . . . ah . . . *know*?

JOSEPH: Of course I didn't know!

NEWSVENDOR: Ah me. And I thought your Mary was such a decent girl, too.

JOSEPH: *(In extreme distress)*: So did I. Oh my goodness!

NEWSVENDOR: It's a sad fact, Mr Carpenter, but I must confess that if my experience of womenfolk is anything to go by – and in my profession you meet all kinds, you really do – you can never –

(But JOSEPH is hurrying off to stage right)

Mr Carpenter? Mr Carpenter – you left your change!

(The NEWSVENDOR shrugs and shakes his head.

As NARRATOR 2 speaks, the SCENERY moves in from left and right to form a line in front of the NEWSVENDOR, who takes his stand and papers off stage right, leaving the chair behind. The SCENERY has arranged itself in a fashion suggestive of a row of houses, with chimneys, roofs, windows, and, towards stage left, a door made up of two individuals standing shoulder to shoulder. A metre or so in front of the line, to stage right, one person with a torch plays a streetlamp)

NARRATOR 2: Mary's husband Joseph, being a just man and unwilling to put her to shame, resolved to divorce her quietly.

NARRATOR 1: A deserted street.

(The SCENERY starts to hum one verse of 'Silent night')

NARRATOR 2: A streetlamp.

(The STREETLAMP switches on the torch. Enter JOSEPH, in the doldrums)

NARRATOR 1: A lonely man going home with a big, big, decision.

(Pausing at the STREETLAMP, JOSEPH peers at his watch. The STREETLAMP helps by redirecting the torch beam, and JOSEPH nods in thanks before turning to open the door. The door squeaks as it swings open. Closing it after him, JOSEPH sits on the chair and starts to snore loudly. By now the humming should just have finished)

NARRATOR 2: That night Joseph slept badly. But this was no ordinary night . . .

(Enter the ANGEL, a sprite, whistling, obviously looking for a house number. Finding the door, he makes to knock, thinks better of it, and after looking this way and that, pulls down the STREETLAMP's arm like a lever, at which the SCENERY disperses to its previous position either side of the stage. The ANGEL now draws the snoring JOSEPH into a mime sequence. He taps him lightly on the shoulder, then holds his pose, awaiting a response)

NARRATOR 1: Joseph Carpenter?

(JOSEPH wakes, looks, then gives a start. He freezes, his eyes fixed on the ANGEL.)

NARRATOR 2: Who are you? said Joseph.

(The ANGEL steps back and takes a deep, introductory bow)

NARRATOR 1: An angel, said the angel.

(Straightening, the ANGEL observes JOSEPH, who having watched the ANGEL bow is staring blankly ahead and running a hand through his hair)

NARRATOR 2: Am I dreaming? said Joseph.

(The ANGEL nods sympathetically and retrieves an imaginary slip of paper from his pocket. This is folded down the centre. The ANGEL takes its edges between thumb and forefinger, and pulls it out flat)

NARRATOR 1: That's right, said the angel. And I've brought a telex for you.

(The ANGEL turns the sheet through ninety degrees

to give JOSEPH a brief view of its contents. JOSEPH glances at it, gives a resigned shrug, and cocks his ear to listen. When the ANGEL presses a fist to his lips to clear his throat the sheet droops, and he has to pull it up again before taking a breath to read. JOSEPH listens intently, a series of surprised expressions passing across his face)

NARRATOR 2: Joseph, son of David, do not fear to take Mary your wife, for that which is conceived in her is of the Holy Spirit; she will bear a son, and call his name Jesus, for he will save his people from their sins.

(After this JOSEPH immediately slaps his knee as if to say 'Of course, I should have realized'. The ANGEL pauses to look at him, simultaneously bringing his thumbs and forefingers together as if to close the telex. JOSEPH clenches one fist and screws up his face)

NARRATOR 1: I knew it, said Joseph.

NARRATOR 2: Knew what? said the angel.

(The ANGEL's question is expressed as an open shrug. JOSEPH extends his arm and points outwards, directing the ANGEL's attention to the 'church', then makes an exasperated throwaway gesture and shakes his head in sorrow)

NARRATOR 1: Knew something was up when she started going to church. Oi veh. Oh, my life.

(The ANGEL steps behind the chair and lays his hands lightly on JOSEPH's shoulders. He smiles down benignly)

NARRATOR 2: But it's all for a good reason, said the angel.

(JOSEPH folds his arms and nods, rolling his eyes up to heaven)

NARRATOR 1: No doubt, said Joseph.

(The ANGEL slaps JOSEPH's shoulders smartly – making JOSEPH wince – and takes a couple of paces to the right. JOSEPH looks at him. The ANGEL beckons vigorously)

NARRATOR 2: No, really, said the angel. Come and look . . .

(The ANGEL takes another two steps to the right and beckons again. JOSEPH glances to his left, back to his right, then gets up, grabs the chair, and follows. As the musical introduction begins to 'God rest you merry, Gentlemen' JOSEPH and the ANGEL stand extreme stage right to watch the dance. At the same time those nearest the back in the two lines of SCENERY move inwards to form the first dancing row. Since, overall, there are three rows – one for each verse of the carol – this row will contain roughly one third of the SCENERY. The steps are the same for everyone, and take the dancers from the back to the front of the stage, where at the end of the verse they immediately divide and return to the sides, moving down the lines to make room for the row following. The accompaniment should be played with a strong rhythm that doesn't lapse between verses. Everybody sings; the steps are given below, the beat numbers for each line indicated in flexed brackets: <>)

(THE DANCE): *(Four steps directly forward, on the beat, starting on 'rest' with the right foot):*

God <1> rest you <2> merry, <3>
gentle<4>men,

(Four steps forward on a left diagonal, starting on 'noth – ' with the right foot):

Let <1> nothing <2> you dis<3>
may, <4>

(Turn to face stage left and take four steps backwards towards stage right, starting on 'know' with the right foot):

You <1> know that <2> Christ our
<3>savi<4> our

(Turn to face audience and sidestep with right foot on 'born', close with left on 'upon'. Repeat with 'day' and the blank beat at the end of the line):

Was <1> born up <2>on this <3>
day, <4>

(Bring left hand to right shoulder on 'save' and right hand to left shoulder on 'Satan's'):

To save us all from Satan's power

(On 'we', bend knees slightly and begin to swing both arms down, out and up in broad arcs, landing both hands on a lowered head on ' – stray'):

When we were gone astray.

(Straighten on 'Oh'. On 'tid – ' touch forehead with right hand, and on ' – ings' extend it fully upwards as though removing and waving a hat. Keeping hand extended, follow it around, rotating in a full circle to the right until facing the audience again on the second 'joy'. Bring right hand down to side):

Oh tidings of comfort and joy,
Comfort and joy,

(Repeat exactly, using left hand for the salute, and turning in a circle to the left):

Oh, tidings of comfort and joy.

(The front row now divides to right and left, leaving the stage free for the second row to come forward on verse 2):

From God our heavenly father
A blessed angel came
And unto certain shepherds
Brought tidings of the same,
How that in Bethlehem was born
The Son of God by name,
Oh, tidings of comfort and joy . . .

(The second row divides to right and left, leaving the stage free for the third row – or, if numbers are short, the first row again – to come forward on verse 3):

Now to the Lord sing praises,
All you within this place,
And with true love and brotherhood
Each other now embrace;
This holy tide of Christmas
All others doth deface,
Oh, tidings of comfort and joy . . .

(At the end of the dance it may be appropriate – if you get it right! – to take a quick bow. Afterwards, the third row goes off to right and left, and the SCENERY resumes its previous position. Enter the NEWSVENDOR with his stand – now reversed and reading 'Census latest')

NEWSVENDOR: *Evening News*! Get your *Evening News*! Long delays in Census registration! All in your *Evening News*!

(JOSEPH comes on from stage right)

NEWSVENDOR: Oh, hello, Mr Carpenter.

JOSEPH: *Evening News*, please.

NEWSVENDOR: Thirty pence. You off to Bethlehem, then?

JOPSEH: Yes – I'm meeting Mary at the station.

NEWSVENDOR: Let us in on the secret, then. What are you going to call the little 'un?

JOSEPH: Jesus.

NEWSVENDOR: Oh. Nice. Even if it's a girl?

JOSEPH: He won't be. You see, I found out what happened. He was conceived by the Holy Spirit.

NEWSVENDOR: You don't say! How d'you know that?

JOSEPH: (*Confiding*): An angel told me. (*He nods and taps his nose with his finger. Then*): Must rush, or I'll be late. See you when I get back.

(JOSEPH leaves in a hurry to stage left)

NEWSVENDOR: Whoa! Your change, Mr Carpenter! *(Seeing he is too late)*: Well I've heard of little birdies telling you things. But angels! I expect he'll come back saying there were whole choirs of them in the clouds singing 'Glory to God in the highest'! Oh well, he's happy.

(The NEWSVENDOR pulls up his coat collar, and rubs his hands together. As NARRATOR 1 is speaking the entire cast moves on to the stage. In a mime, each person greets the NEWSVENDOR, buys a paper – actually a sheet of newspaper folded and cut like a star – and stands facing the audience, feet apart, hands behind his back)

NARRATOR 1: And Joseph went up from Galilee, from the city of Nazareth, to Judea, to the city of David, which is called Bethlehem, because he was of the house and lineage of David to be enrolled with Mary, his betrothed, who was with child. And while they were there, the time came for her to be delivered. And she gave birth to her first-born son and wrapped him in swaddling cloths, and laid him in a manger, because there was no place for them at the inn.

(The cast sings a Christmas song. During an instrumental repeat of the last line, or two lines, everyone makes a half turn clockwise to face the back of

the stage. The stars are unfolded, and on the last beat of the melody the cast completes the clockwise turn and presents a tableau of stars to the audience)

A Jigsaw Tale of Samson

Characters: 5 – 20
Performance time: 2 minutes

This kind of jigsaw can be put together by any group, Sunday school age and up. It may look like Crudens Concordance, but read the parts in order, one line at a time, and you should end up with something resembling a story. Best results are obtained by allocating part FIVE to more than one person.

ONE

● Long ago in Israel,
● long ago in Israel),
● Samson was big
● Every time the Philistines attacked God's people
● But Samson had one weakness:
● Now
● No!
● Lah. Which was an
● Ho hum!
● He married her.
● Sorry. Well, you can guess what happened next.
● How much money
● And
● That night she said to Samson,
● 'Why do you want to know?'
● I mean I'm just curious.'
● said the Philistines when Delilah told them,
● and capture him.'
● Samson leapt up. He snapped the cotton like, er . . .
● said the Philistines.
● And so she nagged him.
● Finally,

●'Okay,' he said,
●'Give me a haircut!'
●'Samson!'
●He couldn't lift it.
●Then they had a feast,
●of Philistines came, so they used the biggest building they had,
●When he'd finished they let him lean against the pillars, to rest.
●And as Samson's hair grew longer and longer he got
●So while the Philistines were all
●Samson put his little finger against one of the pillars
●peeky

TWO

●(in fact,
●there was a man
●and strong,
●Samson would take a donkey's jawbone
●women!
●it just so happened
●Start again!!
●itsy-witsy bit of a
●Never mind!
●Oh no!
●The Philistines came to Delilah
●would you want
●because Delilah was very faithful,
●'Samson, sweetie . . .
●asked Samson. Delilah replied:
●'Well,' said Samson, 'the truth is,
●'In that case,
●So that's what Delilah did.
● – cotton –
●'Samson, you're a meanie,' said Delilah
●Nag.
●Samson
●'Here's my secret.
●So that night,

● Wake up! The Philistines are here!'
● So the Philistines took him away,
● to celebrate.
● with an enormous roof held up by two huge pillars.
● But . . .
● stronger
● boozing
● and gave it a
● infini-

THREE

● very
● whose name
● and did a lot of great things against a lot of nasty people
● and bash them
● And every time Samson saw a woman
● that the best looking woman around
● was called
● problem. Because Delilah was
● So Samson said, 'No thank you, I'll find a wife somewhere else.'
● Oh yes!
● and smiled sweetly
● to betray Samson,
● and loved Samson very much,
● do tell little Delilah
● 'Oh nothing really. It's just –
● if you tie me up with cotton off your sewing machine
● tonight, when Samson's asleep, you tie him up with cotton,
● But when she woke Samson up by screaming:
● (Thank you!)
● 'You promised to tell the truth, and
● Nag, nag,
● gave
● To turn me into a weed
● while Samson was sleeping,
● And Samson leapt up,

● and locked him up.
● Hundreds,
● And they brought Samson in,
● What does hair do
● and stronger
● and woozing
● tiny
● -tessimal

FOUR

● very
● was
● called
● which they didn't like.
● he'd say:
● was called:
● Dee!
● a
● Right?
● Oh, no, no, no.
● and whispered:
● so we can do him in –
● she replied:
● why you're such a hunky
● the Philistines want to kill you.
● I'll turn into a weed.'
● and we'll creep in and say:
● 'Samson! The Philistines are here!'
● picked up his jawbone and
● you lied!
● Nag, nag, nag.
● in.
● all you have to do is . . . '
● Delilah shaved him bald.
● and reached for his jawbone . . .
● click!
● thousands,
● and made him do silly dances for them.
● if you leave it a long time?

● and stronger
● and snoozing
● winy
● little . . .

FIVE

● very
● Samson.
● the Philistines!
● 'Grrr!'
● 'Mmmm!'
● 'Grrr!'
● lie.
● Philistine!
● Wrong!
● Get on with it!
● 'Delilah . . .
● hmmm?'
● 'Fifty pounds!'
● hunk!'
● Whoops!
● 'Ah-hah!'
● 'Grrr!'
● It didn't work!
● 'OUCH!'
● Boo-hoo, blubber, snivel!'
● Nag, nag, nag, nag.
● Trouble!
● 'Yes?'
● Snip, snip, snip!
● *But*
● Heh! heh! heh!
● millions
● Hee! hee! hee!
● It grows!
● and stronger!
● and oozing . . .
● eeky
● push . . .

Big Dollar

Characters: 1 principal, at least 3 others
Performance time: 4 minutes

That God and money are in competition is an idea dating back to the Old Testament prophets. Jesus summed the matter up in Matthew 6:24 – 'No one can serve two masters. Either he will hate the one and love the other, or he will be devoted to the one and despise the other.' Of course, no one whose goal in life is to make a fortune, still less the ordinary person with a three bedroom semi and a pension scheme, would think of himself as 'serving' money, which is why the literal exchange of Mammon and God in BIG DOLLAR seems so absurd. But it does reduce the issue to basics. After all, what are our abiding needs as human beings, and how are they to be satisfied?

The EVANGELIST speaks in a deep Southern accent, and begins the sketch holding a dummy cheque for $100.

(The EVANGELIST stands forward, addressing the audience. Behind him the CHOIR, in close formation, sways gently)

EVANGELIST: Are you ready?

CHOIR: Are you ready!

EVANGELIST: I said, are you *ready*!

CHOIR: Are you *ready*!

EVANGELIST: Oh, I said, are you ready to *go*!

CHOIR: Are you ready to *go*! *(Loudly, breaking*

into applause): Move it, move it! Okay! Get in there!

EVANGELIST: Oh brothers and sisters. You thought you had come to a street show, is that right?

CHOIR (one): It surely is, brother!

EVANGLIST: That's right. Well I'm telling you you have come to more than a street show. You have. Oh people, you have come to a momentous event! You have come to receive riches in abundance!

CHOIR: *(The sound starting to swell)*: Okay! Move, move! Hang in there! Preach it!

EVANGELIST: For this afternoon. This very afternoon. We are giving away what kings and presidents have striven after yet did not attain. We are. We are giving away, money.

CHOIR: Money!

EVANGELIST: Money!

CHOIR: Money!

EVANGELIST: Let's hear it. Get in there! Money!

CHOIR: *Money!*

EVANGELIST: *Not* pizza. *Not* Pink Lilly's elixir. *Not* those little digital alarm clocks made up to look like hamburgers. M, O, N, E, Y, that buys you anything you want!

CHOIR: *(Breaking into applause)*: Ooooooh move over! All right! Preach it. Give it to me, brother, give it to me! Rake it in!

EVANGELIST: *(Suddenly more intimate)*: I tell you, people. One of you here this afternoon is going to take home one, hundred, hot, hot, hot, hot dollars. And all you have to do, is – get, lucky. Let's get out there!

(The CHOIR now disperses and begins to hand out raffle tickets to the audience)

EVANGELIST: Do you feel lucky? I said, do you feel *lucky* this afternoon? If you do, take a number. Take your own, your very own lucky, lucky number. Remember, people, that number is your ticket to ever, lasting, joy. And I don't mean no ordinary joy, I mean joy in the presence of the Big Dollar besides which Sterling, Yen, Deutschmark and all other currencies are but dust and ashes, flotsam and jetsam, pearl and dean. Take that number. Look at it. Cherish it. Commit it to memory. And in just a few short seconds we will tell you if *you* are the chosen one this afternoon.

(The CHOIR has by now returned to its original position. Their responses build again. The EVANGELIST briefly turns his back on the audience, then turns forward again)

Oooh I can feel the inspiration comin'!

CHOIR: Yes.

EVANGELIST: I can feel it comin'!

CHOIR: Yes.

EVANGELIST: It's comin'!

CHOIR: Yes.

EVANGELIST: It's comin'!

CHOIR: Yes!

EVANGELIST: It's comin'!

CHOIR: Yes! Yes! Yes!

EVANGELIST: It's here!

CHOIR: *(With applause)*: All right! Load 'em up, brother! Rake it in! I love it!

EVANGELIST: *(Choosing a number and colour definitely not among those given out)*: On a green ticket, the number is:

ALL: Five, two, one, nine, eight!

EVANGELIST: And who is the lucky person today?

(They all gaze expectantly at the audience. There is, of course, no one with the right ticket)

(If someone tries it on): Yes. Let me see your ticket, sir/madam. Oho! Well I have to applaud your dishonesty, but your technique leaves something to be desired . . . Nobody else? *(If not)*: Well that is the darnedest thing . . . ! He must have just left the meeting . . . Never mind. We are not perplexed. In eventualities like this it is our custom to donate our prize to the needy ones

among us. So may I please call upon the ugliest member of the audience to step forward? *(Somebody just might. If so)*: Is there no depth to which greed will not stoop? Sir/madam, you are an example to us all. *(If not)*: Oh you are coy. You surely are coy this afternoon! In that case we will have to give our valuable prize to this darling li'l boy/girl. *(He chooses someone at random)*: Lil'l boy/girl, would you like just to tell these good folks your name? *(Ignoring the reply)*: Flymo/Angina . . . well isn't that a pretty name? Please, a round of applause for Flymo/Angina.. *(Handing over the cheque)*: Keep the faith, brother/sister. *(Now cranking it up again)*: Okay! Let's hear it for the Big Dollar, people!

CHOIR: The dollar!

EVANGELIST: Money!

CHOIR: Money!

EVANGELIST: The thing we love above all else. And what do we say when we've used it all up?

ALL: *Give – me – more of it!*

CHOIR: *(Break into applause)*

EVANGELIST: *(Rapidly)*: Brothers and sisters, you cannot have too much money. Money is everything. It has no beginning and no end. Money goes on forever. There is no calamity from which you cannot be saved by the power of money, no pit of despair so deep that money cannot raise you up, no place on this earth, be it ever so remote, where money will not open a path before you. Make money your aim and you will be plenteously rewarded. Amen?

CHOIR: Amen!

EVANGELIST: *(Raising a hand in benediction)*: May the power of the Big Dollar overshadow you. May your pockets never be empty, and may your credit never be withdrawn. Stand firm, people. And when the time of trial comes, as it surely will, remember the words of the old pharaoh himself, King Tut: you can't take it with you, but you can have a darn good try . . .

(The performers simultaneously turn their backs on the audience and freeze)

The Seventh Great Cosmic Question

Characters: 4
Performance time: 5 minutes

I called this book ex machina *partly as a mark of respect for the originators of Western theatre – the playwrights of ancient Greece. In those early days it was customary to save an overcomplex plot by winching a god on to the stage (hence* 'deus ex machina'*) and getting him to resolve with a stroke of the divine hand contradictions that in real life would be irresolvable. It has its shortcomings as a dramatic technique; but it foreshadows the intrusion upon the world stage of that far greater machinery we call the Incarnation, and it does, at least, bring the action to a close – a problem playwrights have been struggling with ever since.*

In the Christian context 'closing' suggests not only the end of a performance, but a calling to decision not dissimilar to that for which the same term is used in business marketing. The evangelist closes on his audience by presenting them with a choice, and urging them to make the right decision. But this kind of pressurized ending does not take well to theatre; after all, whatever else he does or says, the performer is there to entertain, and if the actor suddenly turns preacher an audience will rightly feel that its attention has been won on false pretenses.

Of course there are innumerable ways of ending a dramatic performance without either diluting the point you wish to make, or making it so strongly that you only give offence. But there is one longstanding tradition you can always fall back on – passing the hat. The problem is: how to do it without the audience noticing . . .

(The performers – 1, 2, 3 and 4 – stand in a line, right to left)

1: Finally, my colleagues and I would like to thank you for enrolling on our course of practical philosophy. A wise decision! For this morning/afternoon/evening it is our aim to lay bare, once and for all, the deepest mysteries of life.

2: But before we start we'd like to make one thing clear. We do not ask for any gratuities. This priceless information – and it is priceless – will come to you free of charge. *(To the rest)*: Isn't that true?

1, 3, 4: Yes.

2: Tell them. Am I lying?

1, 3, 4: No.

2: Adult or child, rich or poor, you pay nothing whatever. Un*less*, of course . . .

3: Unless you absolutely insist.

2: But we wouldn't dream of asking you.

3: Wouldn't cross our minds – would it?

2: Not in a month of Sundays. If you want to give us money –

1, 2, 3, 4: you'll have to *ask* us!

2: You understand?

1: Good. In that case, on with the lecture.

3: We'll start by going over the basics. Who knows the answer to the First Great Cosmic Question? *(Pausing)*: Anybody over here? *(Feigning amazement)*: *Nobody* knows the answer to the First Great Cosmic Question? *(To the others)*: Well I guess we'll just have to tell them . . .

1, 2, 3, 4: The answer to the First Great Cosmic Question is – *yes!*

3: See, that wasn't so bad, was it? Now – what about the Second Great Cosmic Question? *(Pausing again)*: Nobody knows the answer to the *Second* Great Cosmic question? Who *are* these people? All right . . .

1, 2, 3, 4: The answer to the Second Great Cosmic Question is – *yes!*

3: And the Third Great Cosmic Question –

1, 2, 3, 4:: Yes!

4: And the Fourth –

1, 2, 3, 4: Yes!

2: And the Fifth –

1, 2, 3, 4: Yes!

3: Do we begin to sense a pattern here? All right. Everyone together:

1, 2, 3, 4: The answer to the *Sixth* Great Cosmic Question is . . .

(They cock their ears to the audience, who will respond with a muffled 'Yes'. The performers throw up their hands in despair)

No, no, no.

3: How could you get it wrong? The answer to the Sixth Great Cosmic Question is *no!* It's obvious.

2: Wait a minute. It could be these people haven't ever *asked* the Sixth Great Cosmic Question.

3: What? Never asked . . . ? Oh come on! Everybody's asked the Sixth Great Cosmic Question.

2: They haven't.

3: *(The audience)*: Yes you have! You haven't? I can't believe this!

1: The Sixth Great Cosmic Question is, 'Can I find a public convenience in Britain that hasn't run out of loo paper?'

1, 2, 3, 4: And the answer is:

(The audience reply: 'No!' Whoops and applause from the performers)

2: *(If anybody says 'Yes')*: A miracle – take that person's name.

1: But today we are concerned not with the First, not with the Second, not with the Third, Fourth, Fifth, or Sixth, but with the *Seventh Great Cosmic Question.*

3: Which is so complicated that it takes up most of the Great Cosmic Answer Book.

1, 2, 3: *(Singing a fanfare and pointing at 4, who holds up a small notebook)*: Da, da-da, da, da, da, *daaaah!*

4: *(To the rest)*: Shall we tell them what it is? *(To the audience)*: Shall we? Would you like to know? All right. The Seventh Great Cosmic Question is difficult because it can only be asked in the sacred language of Italiano Mafiosa. But don't worry. What we're going to do is divide you up into four groups and give you one word each. Think you can manage that?

(4 divides the audience, assigning one group to each performer)

The first word is: '*Ont*-a'. Plenty of emphasis on this. '*Ont*-a!' Would the first group like to try that?

(The first group practices. When they have grasped it, 3 rehearses the second group, and so on. The words are, in order: 'ont-a' (as in 'font' – the second syllable barely pronounced), 'da-yew' (as in 'a few', sounding the 'w'), 'utch-a' *(as in 'hutch' – second syllable barely pronounced), and 'howm'. Overall 'ont' and 'utch' have the main stress. 4 makes a lot of the Italian pronunciation*)

Now a little practice run. *(4 orchestrates, ensuring that the words are smoothly connected)*: '*Ont*-a da-yew *utch*-howm.' Again: '*Ont*-a da-yew *utch*-a howm.' *(To the others)*: Oh that was terrific!

1, 2, 3: *(Nodding and applauding)*: Fabulous. Great. The best.

(They smile at the audience, who will be looking nonplussed)

4: Is something wrong? *(making as though to inquire)*: Ah, you don't understand it! Well there's a good reason for that. You see, the vital rule with the language of Italiano Mafiosa is to say every sentence –

1, 2, 3, 4: Backwards!

4: So let's turn it around and see what we can do, eh?

2: And don't forget, though this question is the gateway to the mysteries of life, we ask nothing for telling you what it is!

4: Are you ready? In reverse order . . .

(Again 4 orchestrates. They go twice through the sentence. 'Howm *utch*-a da-yew *ont*-a?', *after which the performers immediately take over)*

1, 2, 3, 4: How much do we want!

1: Do you mean that?

4: How unexpected! *(To 3)*: I'm overcome, aren't you?

3: Yes. This is almost embarrassing.

1: *(To the others)*: What should we say?

2: *(To 1)*: I think fifty pounds should do nicely, don't you?

1: Fifty pounds?

2, 3, 4: *(Nodding)*: Fifty pounds.

1: Fifty it is. May I remind you that we do take cheques, money orders, bank drafts, Access, Visa and American Express, and if you're feeling particularly generous you can throw in your Wimpy chargecard too. Have a nice day . . .

Script Specifications

	1	2	3	4
PRESIDENTS ELECT	*		4	Politics
THE BABBLERS BUILD A TOWER		*	7 +	The Babel story
SANTA WHO?	*		4	Existence of God
RADIO RELIGION	*		6 +	Traditionalism
BOATING FOR GOPHERS	*		4	Noah's Flood
RATTLERS		*	10 +	Regeneration
NOT A NUDIST CLUB			2	Guilt
PIGG			3	Male chauvenism
A HISTORY OF POOKIE	*		5 +	Communication
NO STRINGS	*		4	Giving
THREE WISE PERSONS			3	The miraculous
A SPECIAL CASE			5	Conceit
THE SCOOP			2	The Resurrection
BALLAD OF THE CAKE DIGGERS		*	5 +	Conservation
SHINLICK AND TRASH	*		2	Agnosticism
LONESOME BONESOME		*	8 +	Loneliness (puppet play)
TROUBLE IN ZINGZANG		*	6 +	Disloyalty
YES			2	Marriage
HEROD SEES THE SHRINK			2	The Magi story
A FAMILY PHOTO			14	Family life

DEATH AND RELATED CAUSES			4	Relationship with God
GOOD (EVENING) NEWS		*	12 +	A Nativity play
A JIGSAW TALE OF SAMSON		*	5 +	The Samson story
BIG DOLLAR	*		4 +	Money
THE SEVENTH GREAT COSMIC QUESTION	*		4	Passing the hat

1: Suitable for street theatre
2: Suitable for production by children/young teenagers
3: Minimum cast required
4: Summary of main theme